DATE DUE

MAY 1 4 2010			
APR 1 2013			

Demco, Inc. 38-293

D1416658

Careers in Focus

ELECTRONICS

LIBRARY
MILWAUKEE AREA TECHNICAL COLLEGE
West Campus

621.381
C271

Ferguson
An imprint of Infobase Publishing

Careers in Focus: Electronics

Copyright © 2009 by Infobase Publishing

All rights reserved. No part of this book may be reproduced or utilized in any form or by any means, electronic or mechanical, including photocopying, recording, or by any information storage or retrieval systems, without permission in writing from the publisher. For information contact

Ferguson
An imprint of Infobase Publishing
132 West 31st Street
New York NY 10001

Library of Congress Cataloging-in-Publication Data

Careers in focus. Electronics.
   p. cm.
  Includes index.
  ISBN-13: 978-0-8160-7307-8 (hardcover : alk. paper)
  ISBN-10: 0-8160-7307-4 (hardcover : alk. paper) 1. Electronics—Vocational guidance—Juvenile literature. I. J.G. Ferguson Publishing Company. II. Title: Electronics.
  TK7845.C295 2009
  621.381023—dc22
                       2009003924

Ferguson books are available at special discounts when purchased in bulk quantities for businesses, associations, institutions, or sales promotions. Please call our Special Sales Department in New York at (212) 967-8800 or (800) 322-8755.

You can find Ferguson on the World Wide Web at http://www.fergpubco.com

Text design by David Strelecky
Cover design by Joo Young An

Printed in the United States of America

MP MSRF 10 9 8 7 6 5 4 3 2 1

This book is printed on acid-free paper.

Table of Contents

Introduction

The electronics industry is composed of organizations involved in the manufacture, design and development, assembly, and servicing of electronic equipment and components. Together, these organizations offer a wide variety of products that frequently have only one thing in common: they depend upon electronic technology to operate. Electronics is one of the fastest evolving and most innovative industries, and also one of the most competitive. The research and development of new, better products is of great importance in electronics, where companies often compete fiercely to bring the latest technology to market first.

Electronics is the branch of science and technology that deals with the study, application, and control of the conduction of electricity in a vacuum, in gases, in liquids, in semiconductors, and in conducting and superconducting materials. There are thousands of electronic products with countless applications. These products consist of materials, parts, components, subassemblies, and equipment that use the principles of electronics to perform their major functions.

The products made by the electronics industry can be divided into four basic categories: government products, industrial products, consumer products, and electronic components. The first category, government products, represents a high percentage of sales in the industry. Missile and space guidance systems, communications systems, medical technology, and traffic control devices are just a few of these high-priced, high-tech products.

The second category covers industrial products, which include large-scale computers, radio and television broadcasting equipment, telecommunications equipment, and electronic office equipment. Industrial products also include testing and measuring instruments, industrial control and processing equipment, electronic instruments for nuclear work, and radiation detection devices.

The third category, consumer products, is the most commonly known area and includes such things as wireless phones, compact disc players, DVD players, televisions, radios, and computer and video games. Other consumer products are personal computers, Personal Digital Assistants, electronic ovens and other appliances, and home communications and alarm systems.

The fourth category includes the small pieces that all electronics are made of: components. Integrated circuits, capacitors, switches, transistors, relays, microchips, and amplifiers are among the most widely known.

Today, electronics manufacturing is global in scope. To compete effectively, U.S. electronics suppliers must sell to both domestic and foreign markets. Not only are foreign sales markets vital, but foreign labor markets are increasingly important, too. To stem production expenses, many U.S. electronics manufacturers have moved their assembly and testing plants to other countries where wages are lower. Even so, most manufacturers keep at least part of their operations in the United States. Heavy concentrations of manufacturing plants are located along the Atlantic Coast from Baltimore northward, in the Midwest centering around Chicago, and on the Pacific Coast, with the greatest production center in southern California. One well-known area with a heavy concentration of electronics companies is Silicon Valley, an area south of San Francisco. This area developed with the growth of integrated circuits and microprocessors. During the 1960s and 1970s, many electronic component manufacturers settled their operations there and the area became known as a high-tech area with many companies doing cutting-edge research. Today, some companies are moving from the Silicon Valley and other traditional manufacturing areas to cities in Arizona, Oregon, Texas, and other states. Manufacturing plants are being established in many parts of the country.

There are numerous exciting opportunities and intellectual challenges for the future in electronics manufacturing and associated service operations. New applications are being discovered in such areas as space exploration, telecommunications, computer technology, and industrial and commercial automation. As society becomes increasingly automated at home and at work, the electronics industry will continue to research efficient, innovative ways to incorporate electronics technology into daily life.

Because of its dependence on technology and the need to keep abreast of technical progress, electronics manufacturing provides a large number of opportunities for engineers and scientists. In 2006, approximately 33 percent of individuals working in the electronics industry were in professional specialty occupations, primarily engineers. About 4 percent of those employed in the electronics industry are technicians, mostly electrical and electronics engineering technicians, who work closely with engineers. Today, there is strong growth in companies doing research and development in areas such as telecommunications, computers, and biomedical and medical engineering.

Although electronics employs a high number of professional and technical workers, three out of 10 workers in this field are in production. Many are assemblers, who put together the various parts of an electrical device. Other production workers inspect and test equipment before it is shipped out. About 16 percent of the jobs in this field are finance, managerial, and administrative, and the remainder are clerical and sales and service positions.

Approximately 1.3 million Americans were employed in the computer and electronic product manufacturing industry in 2006. Overall employment in this industry is projected by the U.S. Department of Labor to decline by 12 percent through 2016. The greatest employment declines will occur in the following industry segments: computer and peripheral equipment (-33.5 percent), audio and video equipment (-21.1 percent), and semiconductor and other electronic components (-13.7 percent).

Contributing factors to the decline include the continuing automation of manufacturing processes and the trend for U.S. electronics companies to move their production and assembly operations to lower-wage countries, such as those in the Pacific Rim. Only one industry segment—communications equipment manufacturing (+0.4 percent)—is expected to experience employment growth through 2016.

Growth will also vary among the different types of jobs in the industry. The smallest employment decline is expected among the professional specialty occupations, such as scientists, engineers, and computer systems analysts. This is because of the increasing sophistication of technology and manufacturing processes as well as the competitive nature of the industry, which leads to strong efforts in research and development. Production positions will decline due to increasing technological advancements in manufacturing and outsourcing of positions to plants that are located in foreign countries.

The electronics industry is extremely susceptible to economic conditions, both within the United States and around the world. Global competition is increasing, and many U.S. manufacturers are joining in partnerships with foreign companies in order to succeed. The environment is extremely competitive and is expected to remain so in the future.

Electronics professionals can expect to change jobs and companies several times during their careers. To succeed, professionals will need to acquire multiple skills, pursue advanced education, have a strong technical foundation, and stay up to date on changing technologies.

The articles in *Careers in Focus: Electronics* appear in Ferguson's *Encyclopedia of Careers and Vocational Guidance,* but have been updated and revised with the latest information from the U.S. Department of Labor, professional organizations, and other sources.

The following paragraphs detail the sections and features that appear in this book.

The **Quick Facts** section provides a brief summary of the career including recommended school subjects, personal skills, work environment, minimum educational requirements, salary ranges, certification or licensing requirements, and employment outlook. This section also provides acronyms and identification numbers for the following government classification indexes: the Dictionary of Occupational Titles (DOT), the Guide for Occupational Exploration (GOE), the National Occupational Classification (NOC) Index, and the Occupational Information Network (O*NET)-Standard Occupational Classification System (SOC) index. The DOT, GOE, and O*NET-SOC indexes have been created by the U.S. government; the NOC index is Canada's career classification system. Readers can use the identification numbers listed in the Quick Facts section to access further information about a career. Print editions of the DOT (*Dictionary of Occupational Titles*. Indianapolis, Ind.: JIST Works, 1991) and GOE (*Guide for Occupational Exploration*. Indianapolis, Ind.: JIST Works, 2001) are available at libraries. Electronic versions of the NOC (http://www23.hrdc-drhc.gc.ca) and O*NET-SOC (http://online.onetcenter.org) are available on the Internet. When no DOT, GOE, NOC, or O*NET-SOC numbers are present, this means that the U.S. Department of Labor or Human Resources Development Canada have not created a numerical designation for this career. In this instance, you will see the acronym "N/A," or not available.

The **Overview** section is a brief introductory description of the duties and responsibilities involved in this career. Oftentimes, a career may have a variety of job titles. When this is the case, alternative career titles are presented. Employment statistics are also provided, when available. The **History** section describes the history of the particular job as it relates to the overall development of its industry or field. **The Job** describes the primary and secondary duties of the job. **Requirements** discusses high school and postsecondary education and training requirements, any certification or licensing that is necessary, and other personal requirements for success in the job. **Exploring** offers suggestions on how to gain experience in or knowledge of the particular job before making a firm educational and financial commitment. The focus is on what can be done while still in high school (or in the early years of college) to gain a better understanding of the job. The **Employers** section gives an overview of typical places of employment for the job. **Starting Out** discusses the best ways to land that first job, be it through the college career services office, newspaper ads, Internet employment sites, or personal contact. The **Advancement** section describes what kind of career path to expect from the job and how to get there. **Earnings** lists salary ranges and describes the general fringe benefits. The **Work Environment** section describes the typical surroundings and conditions of employment—whether indoors or outdoors, noisy or quiet, social or independent. Also discussed are typical hours worked, any seasonal fluctuations, and the stresses and strains of the job. The **Outlook** section summarizes the job in terms of the general economy and industry projections. For the most part, Outlook information is obtained from the U.S. Bureau of Labor Statistics and is supplemented by information gathered from professional associations. Job growth terms follow those used in the *Occupational Outlook Handbook*. Growth described as "much faster than the average" means an increase of 21 percent or more. Growth described as "faster than the average" means an increase of 14 to 20 percent. Growth described as "about as fast as the average" means an increase of 7 to 13 percent. Growth described as "more slowly than the average" means an increase of 3 to 6 percent. "Little or no change" means a decrease of 2 percent to an increase of 2 percent. "Decline" means a decrease of 3 percent or more. Each article ends with **For More Information,** which lists organizations that provide information on training, education, internships, scholarships, and job placement.

Careers in Focus: Electronics also includes photos, informative sidebars, and interviews with professionals in the field.

Appliance Service Technicians

OVERVIEW

Appliance service technicians install and service many kinds of electrical and gas appliances, such as washing machines, dryers, refrigerators, ranges, and vacuum cleaners. Some repairers specialize in one type of appliance, such as air conditioners, while others work with a variety of appliances, both large and small, that are used in homes and business establishments. There are approximately 57,000 appliance service technicians employed in the United States.

HISTORY

Although some small home appliances, including irons and coffee makers, were patented before the 20th century began, only a few types were in general use before the end of World War I. Around that time, however, more efficient and inexpensive electric motors were developed, which made appliances more affordable to the general public. In addition, electric and gas utility companies began extending their services into all parts of the nation. As a result, many new labor-saving appliances began to appear on the market. Eventually consumers started to rely increasingly on a wide variety of machines to make everyday tasks easier and more pleasant, both at home and at work. Soon many kinds of equipment, such as washing machines and kitchen ranges, were considered an essential part of middle-class life.

QUICK FACTS

School Subjects
Mathematics
Physics
Technical/shop

Personal Skills
Mechanical/manipulative
Technical/scientific

Work Environment
Primarily indoors
Primarily multiple
  locations

Minimum Education Level
High school diploma

Salary Range
$19,950 to $33,560 to
  $54,190+

Certification or Licensing
Voluntary (certification)
Required by certain states
  (licensing)

Outlook
Little or no change

DOT
827

GOE
05.10.04

NOC
7332

O*NET-SOC
49-2092.00, 49-2092.01,
  49-9031.00, 49-9031.01,
  49-9031.02

Since the end of World War II, there has been a tremendous growth in the use and production of home appliances. The increasing use of appliances has created the need for qualified people to install, repair, and service them. Today's service technicians need a different mix of knowledge and skills than was needed by the appliance repairers of years ago, however, because today's appliances often involve complex electronic parts. The use of electronic components is advantageous to consumers because the electronic appliances are more reliable. However, the fact that modern appliances need fewer repairs means that the demand for appliance technicians is no longer growing as fast as the use of new appliances.

THE JOB

Appliance technicians use a variety of methods and test equipment to figure out what repairs are needed. They inspect machines for frayed electrical cords, cracked hoses, and broken connections; listen for loud vibrations or grinding noises; sniff for fumes or overheated materials; look for fluid leaks; and watch and feel other moving parts to determine if they are jammed or too tight. They may find the cause of trouble by using special test equipment made for particular appliances or standard testing devices such as voltmeters and ammeters. They must be able to combine all their observations into a diagnosis of the problem before they can repair the appliance.

Technicians often need to disassemble the appliance and examine its inner components. To do this, they often use ordinary hand tools like screwdrivers, wrenches, and pliers. They may need to follow instructions in service manuals and troubleshooting guides. To understand electrical circuitry, they may consult wiring diagrams or schematics.

After the problem has been determined, the technician must correct it. This may involve replacing or repairing defective parts, such as belts, switches, motors, circuit boards, or gears. The technician also cleans, lubricates, and adjusts the parts so that they function as well and as smoothly as possible.

Those who service gas appliances may replace pipes, valves, thermostats, and indicator devices. In installing gas appliances, they may need to measure, cut, and connect the pipes to gas feeder lines and to do simple carpentry work such as cutting holes in floors to allow pipes to pass through.

Technicians who make service calls to homes and businesses must often answer customers' questions and deal with their complaints. They may explain to customers how to use the appliance and advise them about proper care. These technicians are often responsible for ordering parts from catalogs and recording the time spent, the parts used, and whether a warranty applies to the repair job. They may need to estimate the cost of repairs, collect payment for their work, and sell new or used appliances. Many technicians who make service calls drive light trucks or automobiles equipped with two-way radios or cellular phones so that as soon as they finish one job, they can be dispatched to another.

Many appliance service technicians repair all different kinds of appliances; there are also those who specialize in one particular kind or one brand of appliances. *Window air-conditioning unit installers and technicians,* for example, work only with portable window units, while *domestic air-conditioning technicians* work with both window and central systems in homes.

Household appliance installers specialize in installing major household appliances, such as refrigerators, freezers, washing machines, clothes dryers, kitchen ranges, and ovens; *household appliance technicians* maintain and repair these units.

Small electrical appliance technicians repair portable household electrical appliances such as toasters, coffee makers, lamps, hair dryers, fans, food processors, dehumidifiers, and irons. Customers usually bring these types of appliances to service centers to have them repaired.

Gas appliance technicians install, repair, and clean gas appliances such as ranges or stoves, heaters, and gas furnaces. They also advise customers on the safe, efficient, and economical use of gas.

REQUIREMENTS

High School

Appliance technicians usually must be high school graduates with some knowledge of electricity (especially wiring diagrams) and, if possible, electronics. If you are interested in this field, you should take as many shop classes as possible to gain a familiarity with machines and tools. Electrical shop is particularly helpful because of the increasing use of electronic components in appliances. Mathematics and physics are good choices to build knowledge of mechanical principles. Computer classes will also be useful.

Postsecondary Training

Prospective technicians are sometimes hired as helpers and acquire most of their skills through on-the-job experience. Some employers assign such helpers to accompany experienced technicians when they are sent to do repairs in customers' homes and businesses. The trainees observe and assist in diagnosing and correcting problems with appliances. Other employers assign helpers to work in the company's service center where they learn how to rebuild used appliances and make simple repairs. At the end of six to 12 months, they usually know enough to make most repairs on their own, and they may be sent on unsupervised service calls.

An additional one to two years of experience is often required for trainees to become fully qualified. Trainees may attend service schools sponsored by appliance manufacturers and also study service manuals to familiarize themselves with appliances, particularly new models. Reading manuals and attending courses is a continuing part of any technician's job.

Many technicians train at public or private technical and vocational schools that provide formal classroom training and laboratory experience in the service and repair of appliances. The length of these programs varies, although most last between one and two years. Correspondence courses that teach basic appliance repair are also available. Although formal training in the skills needed for appliance repair can be a great advantage for job applicants, newly graduated technicians should expect additional on-the-job training to acquaint them with the particular work done in their new employer's service center.

Certification or Licensing

In some states, appliance technicians may need to be licensed or registered. Licenses are granted to applicants who meet certain standards of education, training, and experience and who pass an examination. Since 1994, the Environmental Protection Agency (EPA) has required certification for all technicians who work with appliances containing refrigerants known as chlorofluorocarbons. Since these refrigerants can be harmful to the environment, technicians must be educated and tested on their handling to achieve certification to work with them.

The International Society of Certified Electronics Technicians provides the National Appliance Service Technician Certification Program (NASTeC), which offers certification on four levels: basic skills; refrigeration and air conditioning; cooking; and laundry and dishwashing. Technicians who pass all four exams are certified as NASTeC Universal Technicians.

The Professional Service Association (PSA) also offers certification to appliance repairers. The PSA offers the following certifications to technicians who pass an examination: certified master technician, certified technician, certified service manager, and certified consumer specialist. Certification is valid for four years, at which time technicians must apply for recertification and pass another exami-

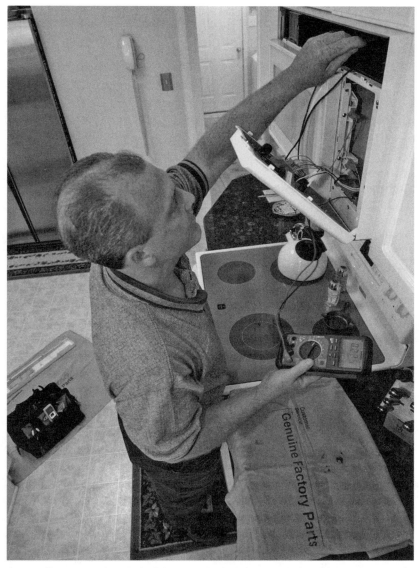

An appliance service technician repairs a microwave oven in a customer's home. *(Erik S. Lesser, AP Photo)*

nation. Certified technicians who complete at least 15 credit hours of continuing education annually during the four years do not need to retake the examination to gain recertification. Additionally, the certified graduate technician designation is available to vocational school graduates who have completed their training. After working for two years as an appliance service technician, holders of this designation can seek to upgrade to the master technician designation.

The North American Retail Dealers Association offers a certification program for those who recover refrigerant from appliances categorized as "Type I" by the EPA. These include refrigerators and freezers designed for home use, room air conditioners including window models, packaged terminal air conditioners, packaged terminal heat pumps, dehumidifiers, under-the-counter icemakers, vending machines, and drinking water coolers. Contact the association for more information on certification requirements.

Other Requirements

Technicians must possess not only the skills and mechanical aptitude necessary to repair appliances, but also skills in consumer relations. They must be able to deal courteously with all types of people and be able to convince their customers that the products they repair will continue to give satisfactory service for some time to come. Technicians must work effectively with little supervision, since they often spend their days alone, going from job to job. It is necessary that they be accurate and careful in their repair work since their customers rely on them to correct problems properly.

EXPLORING

You can explore the field by talking to employees of local appliance service centers and dealerships. These employees may know about part-time or summer jobs that will enable you to observe and assist with repair work. You can also judge interest and aptitude for this

Mean Annual Earnings for Appliance Repairers by Industry, 2007

Natural Gas Distribution	$52,270
Personal and Household Goods Repair and Maintenance	$37,190
Dry-cleaning and Laundry Services	$33,340
Building Equipment Contractors	$33,090
Electronics and Appliance Stores	$32,670

Source: U.S. Department of Labor

work by taking shop courses, especially electrical shop, and assembling electronic equipment from kits.

EMPLOYERS

Currently, there are about 57,000 appliance service technicians employed throughout the United States in service centers, appliance manufacturers, retail dealerships, and utility companies. They may also be self-employed in independent repair shops or work at companies that service specific types of appliances, such as coin-operated laundry equipment and dry-cleaning machines.

STARTING OUT

One way of entering this occupation is to become a helper in a service center where the employer provides on-the-job training to qualified workers. To find a helper's job, prospective technicians should apply directly to local service centers or appliance dealerships. They also can watch area newspaper classified ads for entry-level jobs in appliance service and repair.

For those who have graduated from a technical or vocational program, their schools' career services offices may also prove helpful.

ADVANCEMENT

Advancement possibilities for appliance service technicians depend primarily on their place of employment. In a small service center of three to five people, advancement to a supervisory position will likely be slow, because the owner usually performs most of the supervisory and administrative tasks. However, pay incentives do exist in smaller service centers that encourage technicians to assume a greater share of the management load. Technicians working for large retailers, factory service centers, or gas or electric utility companies may be able to progress to supervisor, assistant service manager, or service manager.

Another advancement route leads to teaching at a factory service training school. A technician who knows the factory's product, works with proficiency, and speaks effectively to groups can conduct classes to train other technicians. Technical and vocational schools that offer courses in appliance repair work may also hire experienced repairers to teach classes.

Some service technicians aspire to opening an independent repair business or service center. This step usually requires a knowledge of business management and marketing and a significant investment in tools, parts, vehicles, and other equipment.

Some technicians who work for appliance manufacturers move into positions where they write service manuals, sell appliances, or act as manufacturers' service representatives to independent service centers.

EARNINGS

The earnings of appliance technicians vary widely according to geographic location, type of equipment serviced, workers' skills and experience, and other factors. In 2007, the U.S. Department of Labor reported that the median annual salary for home appliance technicians was $33,560. At the low end of the salary scale, technicians earned less than $19,950. Technicians at the high end of the pay scale earned $54,190 or more per year. Trainees are usually paid less than technicians who have completed their training period. Employees of gas utility companies and other large companies generally command higher hourly wages than those who work for service centers. Some service centers, however, offer incentives for technicians to increase their productivity. Some of these incentive plans are very lucrative and can allow a proficient worker to add considerably to his or her salary.

Opportunities for overtime pay are most favorable for repairers of major appliances, such as refrigerators, stoves, and washing machines. In addition to regular pay, many workers receive paid vacations and sick leave, health insurance, and other benefits such as employer contributions to retirement pension plans.

WORK ENVIRONMENT

Appliance technicians generally work a standard 40-hour week, although some work evenings and weekends. Repairers who work on cooling equipment, such as refrigerators and air conditioners, may need to put in extra hours during hot weather. In general, there is little seasonal fluctuation of employment in this occupation, since repairs on appliances are needed at all times of the year and the work is done indoors.

Technicians encounter a variety of working conditions depending on the kinds of appliances they install or repair. Those who fix small appliances work indoors at a bench and seldom have to handle heavy objects. Their workplaces are generally well lighted, properly ventilated, and equipped with the necessary tools.

Repairers who work on major appliances must deal with a variety of situations. They normally do their work on-site, so they may spend several hours each day driving from one job to the next. To do repairs, they may have to work in small or dirty spaces or in other uncomfortable conditions. They may have to crawl, bend, stoop, crouch, or lie down to carry out some repairs, and they may have to move heavy items. Because they work in a variety of environments, they may encounter unpleasant situations, such as dirt, odors, or pest infestation.

In any appliance repair work, technicians must follow good safety procedures, especially when handling potentially dangerous tools, gas, and electric currents.

OUTLOOK

The U.S. Department of Labor reports that there will be little or no change in the total number of repairers through 2016. Although Americans will certainly continue buying and using more appliances, today's machines are often made with electronic components that require fewer repairs than their nonelectronic counterparts. Thus, the dependability of the technology built into these new appliances will restrain growth in the repair field. Most openings that arise will be due to workers leaving their jobs who must be replaced. However, the employment outlook will remain very good, with job openings outnumbering job seekers, since relatively few people wish to enter this industry. Opportunities are expected to be best for those with formal training in appliance repair and electronics.

FOR MORE INFORMATION

For information on certification, contact
International Society of Certified Electronics Technicians
3608 Pershing Avenue
Fort Worth, TX 76107-4527
Tel: 800-946-0201
Email: info@iscet.org
http://www.iscet.org

For industry information, contact
National Appliance Service Association
PO Box 2514
Kokomo, IN 46904-2514
Tel: 765-453-1820

Email: nasahq@sbcglobal.net
http://www.nasa1.org

For information on the Refrigerant Recovery Certification Program, contact
North American Retail Dealers Association
222 South Riverside Plaza, Suite 2160
Chicago, IL 60606-6101
Tel: 800-621-0298
Email: nardasvc@narda.com
http://www.narda.com

For information on a career as an appliance service technician and certification, contact
Professional Service Association
71 Columbia Street
Cohoes, NY 12047-2939
Tel: 888-777-8851
http://www.psaworld.com

Avionics Engineers

OVERVIEW

Avionics (from the words *aviation* and *electronics*) is the application of electronics to the operation of aircraft, spacecraft, and missiles. *Avionics engineers* conduct research and solve developmental problems associated with aviation, such as instrument landing systems and other safety instruments. Avionics engineers are a subspecialty of the field of aerospace engineering. There are approximately 90,000 aerospace engineers in the United States.

HISTORY

The field of avionics began in World War II, when military aircraft were operated for the first time using electronic equipment. Rockets were also being developed during this period, and these devices required electronic systems to control their flight. As aircraft rapidly grew more complicated, the amount of electronic apparatus needed for navigation and for monitoring equipment performance greatly increased. The World War II B-29 bomber carried 2,000 to 3,000 avionic components; the B-52 of the Vietnam era carried 50,000; later, the B-58 supersonic bomber required more than 95,000. As the military grew increasingly reliant on electronic systems, specialists were required to build, install, operate, and repair them.

The development of large ballistic missiles during and after World War II and the rapid growth of the U.S. space program after 1958 increased the development of avionics technology. Large missiles and spacecraft require many more electronic components than even the largest and most sophisticated aircraft. Computerized guidance

School Subjects
Mathematics
Technical/shop

Personal Skills
Mechanical/manipulative
Technical/scientific

Work Environment
Primarily indoors
Primarily one location

Minimum Education Level
Bachelor's degree

Salary Range
$53,408 to $90,930 to
$129,770+

Certification or Licensing
Required by all states

Outlook
About as fast as the average

DOT
823

GOE
05.02.01, 05.05.10

NOC
2244

O*NET-SOC
17-2011.00

systems became especially important with the advent of manned spaceflights. Avionics technology was also applied to civil aircraft. The race to be the first in space and, later, to be the first to land on the moon stimulated the need for trained specialists to work with newer and more complex electronic technology. The push for achieving military superiority during the Cold War era also created a demand for avionics specialists and technicians. The commercial airline industry has been growing rapidly since the 1950s; since that time, more and more planes have been built, and the drive to provide greater comfort and safety for passengers has created an even greater demand for avionics engineers and technicians.

Avionics continues to be an important branch of aeronautical and astronautical engineering. The aerospace industry places great emphasis on research and development, assigning a much higher percentage of its trained technical personnel to this effort than is usual in industry. In addition, stringent safety regulations require constant surveillance of in-service equipment. For these reasons there is a high demand for trained and experienced avionics engineers to develop new satellites, spacecraft, aircraft, and their component electronic systems and to maintain those in service.

THE JOB

Avionics engineers develop new electronic systems and components for aerospace use. They also adapt existing systems and components for application in new equipment. For the most part, however, they install, test, repair, and maintain navigation, communications, and control apparatus in existing aircraft and spacecraft.

Avionics engineers involved in the design and testing of a new apparatus must take into account all operating conditions, determining weight limitations, resistance to physical shock, the atmospheric conditions the device will have to withstand, and other factors. For some sophisticated projects, engineers will have to design and make their tools first and then use them to construct and test new avionic components.

The range of equipment in the avionics field is so broad that engineers usually specialize in one area, such as radio equipment, radar, computerized guidance, or flight-control systems. New specialty areas are constantly opening up as innovations occur in avionics. The development of these new specialty areas requires engineers to keep informed by reading technical articles and books and by attending seminars and courses about the new developments, which are often sponsored by manufacturers.

REQUIREMENTS

High School

Persons interested in pursuing a career in avionics should take high school mathematics courses at least through solid geometry and preferably through calculus. They should take English, speech, and communications classes in order to read complex and detailed technical articles, books, and reports; to write technical reports; and to present those reports to groups of people when required. Many schools offer shop classes in electronics and in diagram and blueprint reading.

Postsecondary Training

Avionics engineers must have a bachelor's degree from an accredited college or university and may participate in a cooperative education program through their engineering school.

Larger corporations in the aerospace industry operate their own schools and training institutes. Such training rarely includes theoretical or general studies but concentrates on areas important to the company's functions. The U.S. armed forces also conduct excellent electronics and avionics training schools; their graduates are in high demand in the industry after they leave the service.

Certification or Licensing

All states require engineers to be licensed. There are two levels of licensing for engineers. Professional engineers (PEs) have graduated from an accredited engineering curriculum, have four years of engineering experience, and have passed a written exam. Engineering graduates need not wait until they have four years experience, however, to start the licensure process. Those who pass the Fundamentals of Engineering examination after graduating are called engineers in training (EITs) or engineer interns or intern engineers. The EIT certification usually is valid for 10 years. After acquiring suitable work experience, EITs can take the second examination, the Principles and Practice of Engineering exam, to gain full PE licensure.

To ensure that avionics engineers are kept up to date on their quickly changing field, many states have imposed continuing education requirements for relicensure.

Federal Communications Commission (FCC) regulations require that anyone who works with radio transmitting equipment have a restricted radiotelephone operator's license. Such a license is issued for life upon application to the FCC.

Other Requirements

To be successful in this work, you should have strong science and mathematics skills. In addition, you will need to have good manual dexterity and mechanical aptitude and the temperament for exacting work.

Avionics technicians install electronic equipment on a helicopter. (Reed Saxon, AP Photo)

EXPLORING

One good way to learn more about avionics is to visit factories and test facilities where avionics engineers work as part of teams designing and testing new equipment. You can also arrange to visit other types of electronics manufacturers.

Useful information about avionics training programs and career opportunities is available from the U.S. armed forces as well as from trade and technical schools and community colleges that offer such programs. These organizations are always pleased to answer inquiries from prospective students or service personnel.

EMPLOYERS

Nearly half of the 90,000 aerospace engineers employed in the United States work in the aerospace product and parts manufacturing industries. About 10 percent are employed in federal government agencies, primarily the Department of Defense and the National Aeronautics and Space Administration. Other employers include engineering and architectural services, research and testing services, and search and navigation equipment firms.

STARTING OUT

Those entering the field of avionics must first obtain the necessary training in electronics. Following that training, the school's career services department can help locate prospective employers, arrange interviews, and advise about an employment search. Other possibilities are to contact an employment agency or to approach a prospective employer directly. Service in the military is an excellent way to gain education, training, and experience in avionics; many companies are eager to hire engineers with a military background.

ADVANCEMENT

Avionics engineers are already at an advanced position but may move up to become engineering supervisors or managers. Others may teach avionics at colleges and universities or write about the field for trade publications.

EARNINGS

The U.S. Department of Labor reports that median annual earnings of aerospace/aeronautical/astronautical engineers with a master's degree were $62,459 in 2007. Those with a bachelor's degree earned an average of $53,408 a year, and those with Ph.D.'s earned an average salary of $73,814. Salaries for all aerospace engineers ranged from less than $60,760 to $129,770 or more in 2007. Median annual earnings were $90,930.

Avionics engineers who work for a company usually receive benefits such as vacation days, sick leave, health and life insurance, and a savings and pension program. Self-employed engineers must provide their own benefits.

WORK ENVIRONMENT

Avionics engineers work for aircraft and aerospace manufacturers, airlines, and NASA and other government agencies. Most avionics engineers specialize in a specific area of avionics; they are also responsible for keeping up with the latest technological and industry advances. Their work is usually performed in pleasant indoor surroundings. Because this work is very precise, successful engineers must have a personality suited to meeting exact standards. Engineers sometimes work in closely cooperating teams. This requires an ability to work with a team spirit of coordinated effort.

OUTLOOK

The U.S. Department of Labor predicts that employment for avionics engineers will grow about as fast as the average for all careers through 2016 due to an increase in the number of military aerospace projects and the expected development of new technologies for commercial aircraft.

Avionics is an important and constantly developing field for which more and more trained engineers will be required. Reliance on electronic technology has grown rapidly and in virtually every industry. Many defense contractors have begun to branch out into other products, especially in the areas of electronic and computer technology. Commercial applications of the space program, including the launching of privately owned satellites, are also providing new opportunities in the aerospace industry.

FOR MORE INFORMATION

For a list of accredited colleges and universities, contact
Accreditation Board for Engineering and Technology
111 Market Place, Suite 1050
Baltimore, MD 21202-4102
Tel: 410-347-7700
http://www.abet.org

Contact the AIA for information on aerospace technologies, careers, and space.

Aerospace Industries Association of America (AIA)
1000 Wilson Boulevard, Suite 1700
Arlington, VA 22209-3928
Tel: 703-358-1000
http://www.aia-aerospace.org

For career information and details on student branches of this organization, contact

American Institute of Aeronautics and Astronautics
1801 Alexander Bell Drive, Suite 500
Reston, VA 20191-4344
Tel: 800-639-2422
http://www.aiaa.org

For information on educational programs and to purchase a copy of Engineering: Go For It, contact

American Society for Engineering Education
1818 N Street, NW, Suite 600
Washington, DC 20036-2479
Tel: 202-331-3500
http://www.asee.org

For information on general aviation, contact

General Aviation Manufacturers Association
1400 K Street, NW, Suite 801
Washington, DC 20005-2402
Tel: 202-393-1500
http://www.gama.aero/home.php

For information on careers and student competitions, contact

Junior Engineering Technical Society
1420 King Street, Suite 405
Alexandria, VA 22314-2750
Tel: 703-548-5387
Email: info@jets.org
http://www.jets.org

For career and licensing information, contact

National Society of Professional Engineers
1420 King Street
Alexandria, VA 22314-2794
Tel: 703-684-2800
http://www.nspe.org

For career information, visit the AIAC Web site.
Aerospace Industries Association of Canada (AIAC)
60 Queen Street, Suite 1200
Ottawa, ON K1P 5Y7 Canada
Tel: 613-232-4297
Email: info@aiac.ca
http://www.aiac.ca

—————————————— **INTERVIEW** ——————————————

Thomas Ainsworth works as a digital design engineer in the Space Technology sector, known as NGST, of Northrop Grumman Corporation. He has worked in the field for a little more than four years. Thomas discussed his career with the editors of Careers in Focus: Electronics.

Q. Can you describe a day in your life on the job?
A. My roles have varied quite a bit over the past few years and even in the past few months, so it is difficult to describe a typical day. At a high level though, my day consists mainly of "fire-fighting" and problem-solving. Each day, I come to work and see which fires, or issues, are burning brightest in the morning. Over the past few years, these issues have ranged from missing/late parts to testing failures and troubleshooting. I spend a great deal of time and effort on root-cause investigations. Working in the space industry requires complete mastery of every anomaly and issue. Unlike other industries, there is no possibility of a recall or an on-site repair, so it is important to find the root-cause of any issue with our flight hardware so as to avoid possible on-orbit failures.

In my investigations, I often work with a variety of people. Many times the issues cross beyond the borders of electrical engineering and into other disciplines. In such cases, I depend on my communications skills and basic engineering principles to ultimately solve the issues at hand.

Q. What are the pros and cons of your job?
A. The best part about my job is getting to work with some of the finest engineers in the field and some extraordinary people. Interacting with the many talented folks keeps me excited and makes each day a learning experience.

The primary downside of the job is that I rarely am allowed the opportunity to break out from the problem-solving side and get to work on the front-end in the architecture realm, which I am more interested in. It does get tiresome solving other people's mistakes and problems, when I would much rather be architecting solutions that eliminate the potential problems in the first place.

Q. How/where did you get your first job in this field? What did you do?

A. I actually got my first job in the industry by applying online to NGST. My sister, an aerospace engineer, recommended that I consider the aerospace companies. I had previously been only considering the computer industry, but her suggestion caused me to consider combining my interest in space with my background in computer systems. Fortunately for me, NGST was looking for new computer architects to help in designing computer systems at just the right time.

Q. What are the most important professional and personal qualities for people in your career?

A. There are a number of key qualities for people in my career. Problem-solving, a willingness to learn, and thinking outside of the box are all key to any engineering field. I believe ownership is especially important because it takes ownership of problems/solutions/designs/etc. in order to progress forward and complete tasks. Very little gets done when work is "not my job." The attitude needs to be "it's all our job, and all our responsibility to get it done." Obviously, when people work together, great things can be accomplished.

In terms of personal qualities, flexibility, honesty, and trustworthiness come to mind as some of the most important. In engineering, especially in space where the penalty for failure is so high, it is critical that people are honest and trustworthy. Mistakes must be admitted to lest they cause the loss of a mission, and people must be accountable for their actions. People who live up to their responsibilities are respected, and those who do not will find it very difficult to work on any team.

Q. What advice would you give to high school and college students who are interested in the field?

A. Work is often just plain work, but if you pick a field you enjoy, it can be and should be fun, and then the work is not so boring or frustrating. When the little things get me down, I often try to step back and remember what I am working on and why it is important. My work is directly related to the well-being of my nation and this world. Some of our satellites have spent many years protecting this country. Others are responsible for predicting weather and studying the global climate. Still others have made it possible to understand pieces of the universe that past scientists could hardly conceive. Those things excite me and put my work into perspective. I highly recommend finding a job where the work is fulfilling and exciting because it will greatly help during the inevitable tough times.

Avionics Technicians

OVERVIEW

Avionics (from the words *aviation* and *electronics*) is the application of electronics to the operation of aircraft, spacecraft, and missiles. *Avionics technicians* use their knowledge of electronics to install, repair, test, and service electronic equipment used for navigation, communications, flight control, and other functions in aircraft and spacecraft. Avionics technicians hold about 16,000 jobs in the United States.

HISTORY

The field of avionics emerged during World War II when electronic equipment was first incorporated into military aircraft and rockets. This technology greatly improved navigation, the monitoring of flight performance and systems, and the accuracy of weapons technology.

The growth of the U.S. space program (especially with the advent of manned space flights), the push for achieving military superiority during the Cold War era, and the growth of the commercial airline industry created strong demand for specialists in avionics technology.

Today, avionics technicians are key workers in the aerospace industry—helping to develop electronic systems in spacecraft, satellites, and aircraft.

QUICK FACTS

School Subjects
Mathematics
Technical/shop

Personal Skills
Mechanical/manipulative
Technical/scientific

Work Environment
Primarily indoors
Primarily one location

Minimum Education Level
Some postsecondary training

Salary Range
$33,050 to $48,100 to $63,240+

Certification or Licensing
Voluntary (general technicians)
Required (technicians who work with radio transmitting equipment)

Outlook
About as fast as the average

DOT
823

GOE
05.02.01

NOC
2244

O*NET-SOC
17-3021.00, 49-2091.00

THE JOB

Avionics technicians inspect, test, adjust, and repair the electronic components of aircraft and spacecraft communications, navigation, and flight-control systems and compile complete maintenance and overhaul records for the work they do.

Technicians use apparatus such as circuit analyzers and oscilloscopes to test and replace such sophisticated equipment as transceivers and Doppler radar systems, as well as microphones, headsets, and other standard electronic communications apparatus. New equipment, once installed, must be tested and calibrated to prescribed specifications. Technicians also adjust the frequencies of radio sets and other communications equipment by signaling ground stations and then adjusting set screws until the desired frequency has been achieved. Periodic maintenance checks and readjustments enable avionics technicians to keep equipment operating on proper frequencies. Technicians also complete and sign maintenance and overhaul documents recording the history of various equipment.

Technicians may be involved in the design and development of new electronic equipment. They must consider operating conditions, including weight limitations, resistance to physical shock, atmospheric conditions the device will have to withstand, magnetic field interference, and other crucial factors. Avionics technicians in research and development must anticipate potential problems and rigorously test the new components.

Avionics technicians usually work as part of a team, especially if involved in research, testing, and development of new products. They are often required to keep notes and records of their work and to write detailed reports.

REQUIREMENTS

High School

A solid educational background in mathematics (at least through solid geometry and preferably through calculus) and electronics is the most crucial element if you want to become an avionics technician. As an avionics technician, you will read schematics and diagrams, so a blueprint reading or drawing class will come in handy. Take English and speech classes because it is important to be able to write and read technical reports and to communicate clearly with others both verbally and in writing.

Postsecondary Training

Avionics technicians must have completed a course of training at a postsecondary technical institute or community college. The program should include at least one year of electronics technician training. If not trained specifically in avionics, students should obtain a solid background in electronics theory and practice. Further specialized training will be done on the job, where technicians work with engineers and senior technicians until they are competent to work without direct supervision. The U.S. armed forces also offer excellent electronics and avionics training.

Certification or Licensing

The Electronics Technicians Association, International (ETA) offers four levels of voluntary certification (Certified Associate, Journeyman, Senior, and Master) for electronics service technicians who wish to specialize in avionics. To become certified, technicians must have a specified number of years of work and/or electronics training and pass an examination. Contact the ETA for more information. Avionics technicians may also need to obtain a mechanics certificate from the Federal Aviation Administration.

The Federal Communications Commission (FCC) requires that anyone who works with radio transmitting equipment have a restricted radiotelephone operator's license. Such a license is issued for life upon application to the FCC.

Other Requirements

To be successful in this field, you must have excellent analytical and problem-solving skills. Self-motivation, persistence, and the ability to follow through on projects are important as well. You should also have strong mathematics and science skills. In addition, you will need to have good manual dexterity and mechanical aptitude.

EXPLORING

An excellent way to learn more about this field is to visit factories and test facilities where avionics technicians work as part of teams designing and testing new equipment. If possible, visit a large airfield's repair facilities where avionics technicians inspect, maintain, and calibrate communications and control apparatus. You can also ask your guidance counselor to help arrange an information interview with an avionics technician and visit the Web sites of professional associations for more information.

EMPLOYERS

Approximately 16,000 avionics technicians are employed in the United States. Most technicians work for airlines or airports and flying fields. Other major employers include the federal government (including the National Aeronautics and Space Administration, or NASA) and aircraft assembly firms.

STARTING OUT

Counselors at college career service offices can help students locate job openings. Schools frequently host job fairs where students can meet prospective employers. Professional associations and companies also often offer employment listings at their Web sites. Service in the military is an excellent way to gain education, training, and experience in avionics; visit Today's Military (http://www.todays military.com) for more information.

ADVANCEMENT

Avionics technicians usually begin their careers in trainee positions until they are thoroughly familiar with the requirements and routines of their work. Having completed their apprenticeships, they are usually assigned to work independently, with only minimal supervision, doing testing and repair work. The most experienced and able technicians go on to install new equipment and to work in research and development operations. Many senior technicians move into training, supervisory, sales, and customer relations positions. Some choose to pursue additional training and become avionics engineers.

EARNINGS

Median earnings of avionics technicians were $48,100 in 2007, according to the U.S. Department of Labor. The top 10 percent of technicians earned more than $63,240 a year. The lowest 10 percent earned less than $33,050 a year. Federal government employees (not including armed forces personnel) on the average earn slightly less than avionics technicians employed by private aerospace firms. Their jobs, however, are more secure.

Benefits for full-time workers include vacation and sick time, health, and sometimes dental, insurance, and pension or 401(k) plans. Self-employed avionics technicians must provide their own benefits.

WORK ENVIRONMENT

Avionics technicians may work in a pleasant shop atmosphere on individual pieces or equipment or outdoors on large aircraft. Because the range of equipment in the avionics field is so broad, avionics technicians may specialize in a specific area of avionics (such as computerized guidance equipment, flight-control systems, or radio equipment). As a result, they must keep up with the latest technological and industry advances by continuing to learn throughout their careers.

OUTLOOK

The U.S. Department of Labor (USDL) predicts that employment for avionics technicians should grow as fast as the average for all occupations through 2016. There will always be a need for skilled avionics technicians. The USDL reports that technicians who have been trained to work on complex aircraft systems or who have been licensed to work on the entire aircraft—not just the electronics systems—will have the strongest employment opportunities.

FOR MORE INFORMATION

For industry information, contact the following organizations:
Aerospace Industries Association
1000 Wilson Boulevard, Suite 1700
Arlington, VA 22209-3928
Tel: 703-358-1000
http://www.aia-aerospace.org

General Aviation Manufacturers Association
1400 K Street, NW, Suite 801
Washington, DC 20005-2402
Tel: 202-393-1500
http://www.gama.aero/home.php

For career information and details on student branches of this organization, contact
American Institute of Aeronautics and Astronautics
1801 Alexander Bell Drive, Suite 500
Reston, VA 20191-4344
Tel: 800-639-2422
http://www.aiaa.org

For information on certification, contact
Electronics Technicians Association, International
5 Depot Street
Greencastle, IN 46135-8024
Tel: 800-288-3824
Email: eta@eta-i.org
http://www.eta-i.org

For information on aviation careers and scholarships, contact
National Air Transportation Association
4226 King Street
Alexandria, VA 22302-1507
Tel: 800-808-6282
http://www.nata.aero

For career information, visit the AIAC Web site.
Aerospace Industries Association of Canada (AIAC)
60 Queen Street, Suite 1200
Ottawa, ON K1P 5Y7 Canada
Tel: 613-232-4297
Email: info@aiac.ca
http://www.aiac.ca

College Professors, Electrical Engineering

OVERVIEW

The discipline of electrical engineering focuses on the development of equipment that produces and distributes electricity, such as generators, transmission lines, and transformers. It centers on the creation of devices made up of electronic components, such as integrated circuits and microprocessors. Electronics engineering is a subfield of electrical engineering, and both types of engineers are often referred to as electrical engineers. *Electrical engineering professors* instruct undergraduate and graduate students in the subjects of electrical, electronics, and computer engineering at colleges and universities. They lecture classes, lead small seminar groups, and create and grade examinations. They also may conduct research, write for publication, and aid in administration. There are approximately 32,300 engineering teachers at the postsecondary level.

HISTORY

The concept of colleges and universities goes back many centuries. These institutions evolved slowly from monastery schools, which trained a select few for certain professions, notably theology. The terms *college* and *university* have become virtually interchangeable in America outside the walls of academia, although originally they designated two very different kinds of institutions.

Two of the most notable early European universities were the University of Bologna in Italy, thought to have been established in

QUICK FACTS

School Subjects
Computers
English
Speech

Personal Skills
Communication/ideas
Helping/teaching

Work Environment
Primarily indoors
Primarily one location

Minimum Education Level
Master's degree

Salary Range
$43,090 to $79,510 to
$133,920+

Certification or Licensing
None available

Outlook
Much faster than the average

DOT
090

GOE
11.02.01

NOC
4121

O*NET-SOC
25-1032.00

the 12th century, and the University of Paris, which was chartered in 1201. These universities were considered to be models after which other European universities were patterned. Oxford University in England was probably established during the 12th century. Oxford served as a model for early American colleges and universities and today is still considered one of the world's leading institutions.

Harvard, the first U.S. college, was established in 1636. Its stated purpose was to train men for the ministry; the early colleges were all established for religious training. With the growth of state-supported institutions in the early 18th century, the process of freeing the curriculum from ties with the church began. The University of Virginia established the first liberal arts curriculum in 1825, and these innovations were later adopted by many other colleges and universities.

Although the original colleges in the United States were patterned after Oxford University, they later came under the influence of German universities. During the 19th century, more than 9,000 Americans went to Germany to study. The emphasis in German universities was on the scientific method. Most of the people who had studied in Germany returned to the United States to teach in universities, bringing this objective, factual approach to education and to other fields of learning.

In 1833, Oberlin College in Oberlin, Ohio, became the first college founded as a coeducational institution. In 1836, the first women-only college, Wesleyan Female College, was founded in Macon, Georgia.

The junior college movement in the United States has been one of the most rapidly growing educational developments. Junior colleges first came into being just after the turn of the 20th century.

The first electrical engineering program in the world was founded at Cornell University in 1883. Ten years later, the American Society for Engineering Education was founded to represent the professional interests of engineering educators. Today, many colleges and universities offer electrical engineering-related majors. More than 440 of these programs are accredited by the Accreditation Board for Engineering Technology.

THE JOB

Electrical engineering faculty members teach at junior colleges or at four-year colleges and universities. At four-year institutions, most faculty members are *assistant professors, associate professors,* or *full professors.* These three types of professorships differ in regards to status, job responsibilities, and salary. Assistant professors are new faculty members who are working to get tenure (status as a permanent professor); they seek to advance to associate and then to full professorships.

Electrical engineering professors perform three main functions: teaching, advising, and research. Their most important responsibility is to teach students. Their role within the department will determine the level of courses they teach and the number of courses per semester. Most professors work with students at all levels, from college freshmen to graduate students. They may head several classes a semester or only a few a year. Some of their classes will have large enrollments, while graduate seminars may consist of only 12 or fewer students. Though professors may spend fewer than 10 hours a week in the actual classroom, they spend many hours preparing lectures and lesson plans, grading papers and exams, and preparing grade reports. They also schedule office hours during the week to be available to students outside of the lecture hall, and they meet with students individually throughout the semester. In the classroom, professors lecture, lead discussions, administer exams, and assign textbook reading and other research. While many professors teach entry-level classes such as "Elements of Electrical Engineering," "Introductory Electromagnetics," "Electric Circuit Analysis" or "Engineering Physics," some also teach graduate-level classes. Others teach concentrations that center on a particular specialty, such as wireless electrical engineering or communications, networks, and systems. In some courses, they rely heavily on computer laboratories to teach course material.

Another important responsibility is advising students. Not all faculty members serve as advisers, but those who do must set aside large blocks of time to guide students through the program. College professors who serve as advisers may have any number of students assigned to them, from fewer than 10 to more than 100, depending on the administrative policies of the college. Their responsibility may involve looking over a planned program of studies to make sure the students meet requirements for graduation, or it may involve working intensively with each student on many aspects of college life. They may also discuss the different career paths in electrical and electronics engineering with students and help them identify the best career choices.

The third responsibility of college and university faculty members is research and publication. Faculty members who are heavily involved in research programs sometimes are assigned a smaller teaching load. College electrical engineering professors publish their research findings in various scholarly journals such as *EE Times*, the *Journal on Emerging Technologies in Computing Systems*, and

Computing in Science & Engineering. They also write books based on their research or on their own knowledge and experience in the field. Most textbooks are written by college and university teachers, or veterans of the computer industry or engineering firms. Publishing a significant amount of work has been the traditional standard by which assistant professors prove themselves worthy of becoming permanent, tenured faculty. Typically, pressure to publish is greatest for assistant professors. Pressure to publish increases again if an associate professor wishes to be considered for a promotion to full professorship.

Some faculty members eventually rise to the position of *department chair,* where they govern the affairs of an entire electrical engineering department. Department chairs, faculty, and other professional staff members are aided in their myriad duties by *graduate assistants,* who may help develop teaching materials, moderate laboratories and workshops, conduct research, give examinations, teach lower-level courses, and carry out other activities.

Some electrical engineering professors may also conduct classes in an extension program. In such a program, they teach evening and weekend courses for the benefit of people who otherwise would not be able to take advantage of the institution's resources. They may travel away from the campus and meet with a group of students at another location. They may work full time for the extension division or may divide their time between on-campus and off-campus teaching.

Distance learning programs, an increasingly popular option for students, give professors the opportunity to use today's technologies to remain in one place while teaching students who are at a variety of locations simultaneously. The professor's duties, like those when teaching correspondence courses conducted by mail, include grading work that students send in at periodic intervals and advising students of their progress. Computers, the Internet, email, and video conferencing are some of the technology tools that allow professors and students to communicate in "real time" in a virtual classroom setting. Meetings may be scheduled during the same time as traditional classes or during evenings and weekends. Professors who do this work are sometimes known as *extension work, correspondence,* or *distance learning instructors.* They may teach online courses in addition to other classes or may have distance learning as their major teaching responsibility.

The *junior college instructor* has many of the same kinds of responsibilities as does the teacher in a four-year college or university. Because junior colleges offer only a two-year program, they teach only undergraduates. These programs typically offer certificates and associate's degrees in electrical/electronics technology,

A college professor uses a diagram to make a point in class. *(Sonda Dawes, The Image Works)*

electronics and computer engineering, or general engineering or engineering technology.

REQUIREMENTS

High School

Your high school's college preparatory program likely includes courses in computer science, English, science, foreign language, history, and mathematics. In addition, you should take courses in speech to get a sense of what it will be like to lecture to a group of students. Your school's debate team can also help you develop public speaking skills along with research skills.

Postsecondary Training

At least one advanced degree in electrical engineering, computer engineering, or a related field is required to be an electrical engineering professor in a college or university. The master's degree is considered the minimum standard, and graduate work beyond the master's is usually desirable. If you hope to advance in academic rank above instructor, most institutions require a doctorate. Many large universities and colleges have a strong preference for those with a Ph.D. in electrical engineering or a closely related field. Visit the Accreditation Board for Engineering and Technology's Web site, http://www.abet.org, for a list of accredited programs.

In the last year of your undergraduate program, you'll apply to graduate programs in your area of study. Standards for admission to a graduate program can be high and the competition heavy, depending on the school. Once accepted into a program, your responsibilities will be similar to those of your professors—in addition to attending seminars, you'll research, prepare articles for publication, and teach some undergraduate courses.

You may find employment in a junior college with only a master's degree. Advancement in responsibility and in salary, however, is more likely to come if you have earned a doctorate.

Other Requirements

To be a successful professor, you should enjoy reading, writing, and researching. Not only will you spend many years studying in school, but your whole career will be based on communicating your thoughts and ideas, as well as abstract concepts to students. People skills are important because you'll be dealing directly with students, administrators, and other faculty members on a daily basis. You should feel comfortable in a role of authority and possess self-confidence.

EXPLORING

Learn as much as you can about engineering. Visit Web sites and read books and magazines that relate to engineering. Some of the more popular engineering sites for teens include the Junior Engineering Technical Society (http://www.jets.org) and American Society for Engineering Education Engineering K12 Center (http://www.asee.org/k12).

Your high school teachers use many of the same skills as electrical engineering professors, so talk to your teachers about their careers and their college experiences. You can develop your own teaching experience by volunteering at a community center, working at a day care center, or working at a summer camp. Also, spend some time on a college campus to get a sense of the environment. Write to colleges for their admissions brochures and course catalogs (or check them out online); read about the faculty members and the courses they teach. Before visiting college campuses, make arrangements to speak to professors who teach courses that interest you. These professors may allow you to sit in on their classes or labs and observe. Also, make appointments with college advisers and with people in the admissions and recruitment offices. If your grades are good enough, you might be able to serve as a teaching assistant during your undergraduate years, which can give you experience leading discussions and grading papers.

EMPLOYERS

Approximately 32,300 engineering faculty are employed in the United States. Employment opportunities vary based on area of study and education. Most universities have many different departments that hire faculty. With a doctorate, a number of publications, and a record of good teaching, professors should find opportunities in universities all across the country. Professors teach in undergraduate and graduate programs. The teaching jobs at doctoral institutions are usually better paying and more prestigious. The most sought-after positions are those that offer tenure. Teachers who have only a master's degree will be limited to opportunities with junior colleges, community colleges, and some small private institutions.

STARTING OUT

You should start the process of finding a teaching position while you are in graduate school. The process includes developing a curriculum vitae (a detailed, academic resume), writing for publication, assisting with research, attending conferences, and gaining teaching experience and recommendations. Many students begin applying for teaching positions while finishing their graduate program. For most positions at four-year institutions, you must travel to large conferences where interviews can be arranged with representatives from the universities to which you have applied.

Because of the competition for tenure-track positions, you may have to work for a few years in temporary positions, visiting various schools as an *adjunct professor*. Some professional associations maintain lists of teaching opportunities in their areas. They may also make lists of applicants available to college administrators looking to fill an available position.

Some professors begin teaching after having successful careers as electrical engineers.

ADVANCEMENT

The normal pattern of advancement is from instructor to assistant professor, to associate professor, to full professor. All four academic ranks are concerned primarily with teaching and research. College faculty members who have an interest in and a talent for administration may be advanced to department chair or dean of their college. A few become college or university presidents or other types of administrators.

The instructor is usually an inexperienced college teacher. He or she may hold a doctorate or may have completed all the Ph.D. requirements except for the dissertation. Most colleges look upon the rank of instructor as the period during which the college is trying out the teacher. Instructors usually are advanced to the position of assistant professors within three to four years. Assistant professors are given up to about six years to prove themselves worthy of tenure, and if they do so, they become associate professors. Some professors choose to remain at the associate level. Others strive to become full professors and receive greater status, salary, and responsibilities.

Most colleges have clearly defined promotion policies from rank to rank for faculty members, and many have written statements about the number of years in which instructors and assistant professors may remain in grade. Administrators in many colleges hope to encourage younger faculty members to increase their skills and competencies and thus to qualify for the more responsible positions of associate professor and full professor.

EARNINGS

According to the U.S. Department of Labor, in 2007, the median salary for all engineering postsecondary instructors was $79,510, with 10 percent earning $133,920 or more and 10 percent earning $43,090 or less. Those with the highest earnings tend to be senior tenured faculty; those with the lowest, graduate assistants. Professors working on the West Coast and the East Coast and those working at doctorate-granting institutions also tend to earn the highest salaries. Many professors try to increase their earnings by completing research, publishing in their field, or teaching additional courses.

Benefits for full-time faculty typically include health insurance and retirement funds and, in some cases, stipends for travel related to research, housing allowances, and tuition waivers for dependents.

WORK ENVIRONMENT

A college or university is usually a pleasant place in which to work. Campuses bustle with all types of activities and events, stimulating ideas, and a young, energetic population. Much prestige comes with success as a professor and scholar; professors have the respect of students, colleagues, and others in their community.

Depending on the size of the department, electrical engineering professors may have their own office, or they may have to share an office with one or more colleagues. Their department may provide them with a computer, Internet access, and research assistants. College professors are also able to do much of their office work at home. They can arrange their schedule around class hours, academic meetings, and the established office hours when they meet with students. Most electrical engineering teachers work more than 40 hours each week. Although professors may teach only two or three classes a semester, they spend many hours preparing for lectures, examining student work, and conducting research.

OUTLOOK

The U.S. Department of Labor predicts much faster than average employment growth for college and university professors through 2016. College enrollment is projected to grow due to an increased number of 18- to 24-year-olds, an increased number of adults returning to college, and an increased number of foreign-born students. Retirement of current faculty members will also provide job openings. However, competition for full-time, tenure-track positions at four-year schools will be very strong.

Employment for electrical and electronics engineers is expected to grow more slowly than the average for all occupations through 2016, according to the *Occupational Outlook Handbook*. Despite this prediction, there should continue to be strong opportunities for electrical engineering professors as enrollments in electrical engineering programs continue to grow.

FOR MORE INFORMATION

To read about the issues affecting college professors, contact the following organizations:

42 Careers in Focus: Electronics

American Association of University Professors
1133 19th Street, NW, Suite 200
Washington, DC 20036-3604
Tel: 202-737-5900
Email: aaup@aaup.org
http://www.aaup.org

American Federation of Teachers
555 New Jersey Avenue, NW
Washington, DC 20001-2029
Tel: 202-879-4400
Email: online@aft.org
http://www.aft.org

For information on careers, contact
American Society for Engineering Education
1818 N Street, NW, Suite 600
Washington, DC 20036-2479
Tel: 202-331-3500
http://www.asee.org

For employment information, links to online career sites, information on membership for college students, and background on the industry, contact
Institute of Electrical and Electronics Engineers (IEEE-USA)
2001 L Street, NW, Suite 700
Washington, DC 20036-4910
Tel: 202-785-0017
Email: ieeeusa@ieee.org
http://www.ieeeusa.org

For comprehensive information about careers in electrical engineering and computer science, visit
Sloan Career Cornerstone Center
http://careercornerstone.org

INTERVIEW

Dr. Tomás Palacios is an assistant professor of electrical engineering and leader of the Widebandgap Semiconductor Materials and Devices Group at the Massachusetts Institute of Technology (MIT) in Cambridge, Massachusetts. He discussed his career with the editors of Careers in Focus: Electronics.

Q. Tell us about yourself and your work with the Wideband-gap Semiconductor Materials and Devices Group.

A. I am originally from Madrid, Spain, where I studied telecommunication engineering, the Spanish equivalent to electrical engineering and computer science. In 2002, I came to the United States to get a Ph.D. from the University of California at Santa Barbara. Since 2006 I have been an assistant professor of electrical engineering at MIT where my group, the Widebandgap Semiconductor Materials and Devices Group, works on pushing the limits of electronics. We work on transistors, small switches that are the main building blocks of electronics. We aim to make them 1000 times faster than the ones used in conventional computers. We also develop electronic circuits that can work at extreme temperatures such as the 600°C found on the surface of Mercury and new electronic devices that can revolutionize the way we use energy.

Q. What is one thing that young people may not know about a career in electrical engineering?

A. Electrical engineering gives a very broad education that opens the doors to many fields. Electrical engineers are today inventing the Internet of the future, designing the next iPhone, changing the way we use energy, and developing new methods to sequence the entire human genome for just a few dollars. The possibilities for a career in electrical engineering are very broad and limitless.

Q. What classes do you currently teach and what level of students?

A. I am currently teaching MIT 6.012 (Microelectronic Devices and Circuits). This class is an intermediate-level course on electronic devices and circuits for sophomore students. In this class, students learn about the structure of electronic circuits and how to build them. It is a very interesting course where the students start with very little knowledge of electronics and leave knowing why the microprocessor in their computers is made in the way it is.

Q. What advice would you offer electrical engineering majors as they graduate and look for jobs?

A. Important advice is that they should always keep their eyes open. Electrical engineering is continuously reinventing itself at an amazing speed. It is very different from what we had 100 years ago and, in the future, it will be very different from what we have today. The electrical engineering education prepares you to adapt to these changes, and it is a lot of fun to witness these changes and play a role in them. But if you want to be ready for the changes, you should always keep your eyes open, never stop learning, and don't be worried to think differently.

Q. What are some of the pros and cons of your job?

A. I sincerely think I have the best job in the world. Teaching is extremely rewarding and, at the same time, I am very fortunate to be involved in cutting-edge research with amazing students and colleagues. Electrical engineering is in the middle of the crossroads where electronics, information technology, biology, and energy are coming together. Now is a tremendously exciting and fun time to be working in this field. I wish days would have 48 hours to be able to take advantage of all the opportunities.

It is very difficult for me to identify any drawback of my job. The only thing I can think of is that I have to spend a lot of time on a plane, traveling to attend scientific conferences, review meetings, or to meet sponsors. However, it is not that bad and at the end you get used to it and you have a chance to visit some really amazing places.

Q. What has been your most rewarding professional experience and why?

A. I find it extremely rewarding each time one of my students comes to me with a problem that seems impossible at first. Then, after a few minutes/hours working together, we succeed to find the way to solve it. As engineers we should always try to make the impossible possible, and it feels really good when we do it. Also, it is a wonderful experience to know that you are doing things that nobody else has ever tried and developing new ideas that will enable breakthroughs in how we transmit information or how we use energy. In addition, to do all this in collaboration with extremely talented colleagues and students at MIT is really rewarding.

Computer-Aided Design Drafters and Technicians

OVERVIEW

Computer-aided design drafters and technicians, sometimes called *CAD technicians* or *CAD designers,* use computer-based systems to produce or revise technical illustrations needed in the design and development of machines, electronic components, products, buildings, manufacturing processes, and other work. They use CAD machinery to manipulate and create design concepts so that they are feasible to produce and use in the real world.

HISTORY

Just over 30 years ago, drafting and designing were done with a pencil and paper on a drafting table. To make a circle, drafters used a compass. To draw straight lines and the correct angles, they used a straight-edge, T-square, and other tools. With every change required before a design was right, it was "back to the drawing board" to get out the eraser, sharpen the pencil, and revise the drawing. Everybody did it this way, whether the design was simple or complex: automobiles, hammers, printed circuit boards, utility piping, highways, or buildings.

CAD technology came about in the 1970s with the development of microprocessors (computer processors in the form of miniaturized integrated circuits

QUICK FACTS

School Subjects
Computer science
Mathematics
Technical/shop

Personal Skills
Mechanical/manipulative
Technical/scientific

Work Environment
Primarily indoors
Primarily one location

Minimum Education Level
Some postsecondary
training

Salary Range
$27,680 to $45,000 to
$77,530+

Certification or Licensing
Voluntary

Outlook
More slowly than the
average

DOT
003

GOE
02.08.03

NOC
2253

O*NET-SOC
17-3011.01, 17-3011.02,
17-3012.01, 17-3012.02,
17-3013.00

contained on tiny silicon chips). Microprocessors opened up many new uses for computers by greatly reducing the size of computers while also increasing their power and speed.

Interestingly, the drafters and designers working to develop these microprocessors were also the first to benefit from this technology. As the circuits on the silicon chips that the designers were working on became too complex to diagram by pencil and paper, the designers began to use the chips themselves to help store information, create models, and produce diagrams for the design of new chip circuits. This was just the beginning of computer-assisted design and drafting technology. Today, there are tens of thousands of CAD workstations in industrial settings. CAD systems greatly speed up and simplify the designer's and drafter's work. They do more than just let the operator "draw" the technical illustration on the screen. They add the speed and power of computer processing, plus software with technical information that ease the designer/drafter's tasks. CAD systems make complex mathematical calculations, spot problems, offer advice, and provide a wide range of other assistance. Today, nearly all drafting tasks are done with such equipment.

As the Internet has developed, CAD operators can send a CAD drawing across the world in a matter of minutes attached to an email message. Gone are the days of rolling up a print and mailing it. Technology has once again made work more efficient for the CAD designer and drafter.

THE JOB

Technicians specializing in CAD technology usually work in the design and drafting activities associated with new product research and development, although many work in other areas such as structural mechanics or piping. CAD technicians must combine drafting and computer skills. They work in any field where detailed drawings, diagrams, and layouts are important aspects of developing new product designs—for example, in architecture, electronics, and in the manufacturing of automobiles, aircraft, computers, and missiles and other defense systems. Most CAD technicians specialize in a particular industry or on one part of a design.

CAD technicians work under the direction and supervision of *CAD engineers and designers,* experts highly trained in applying computer technology to industrial design and manufacturing. These designers and engineers plan how to relate the CAD technology and equipment to the design process. They are also the ones who give assignments to the CAD technicians.

Jackie Sutherland started as a drafter right out of high school, working at a major Midwestern diesel engine manufacturer. Since then, he has moved into a designer's role. In his 25 years on the job, he has seen the transfer from drafting table to CAD workstation.

"I work with everyone from the customer to the engineers, suppliers, pattern makers, and the assembly line from the project concept through the production," says Sutherland of his work as a CAD designer.

Technicians work at specially designed and equipped interactive computer graphics workstations. They call up computer files that hold data about a new product; they then run the programs to convert that information into diagrams and drawings of the product. These are displayed on a display screen, which then acts as an electronic drawing board. Following the directions of a CAD engineer or designer, the CAD technician enters changes to the product's design into the computer. The technician merges these changes into the data file, then displays the corrected diagrams and drawings.

The software in CAD systems is very helpful to the user—it offers suggestions and advice and even points out errors. The most important advantage of working with a CAD system is that it saves the technician from the lengthy process of having to produce, by hand, the original and then the revised product drawings and diagrams.

The CAD workstation is equipped to allow technicians to perform calculations, develop simulations, and manipulate and modify the displayed material. Using typed commands at a keyboard, a stylus or light pen for touching the screen display, a mouse, joystick, or other electronic methods of interacting with the display, technicians can move, rotate, or zoom in on any aspect of the drawing on the screen, and project three-dimensional images from two-dimensional sketches. They can make experimental changes to the design and then run tests on the modified design to determine its qualities, such as weight, strength, flexibility, and the cost of materials that would be required. Compared to traditional drafting and design techniques, CAD offers virtually unlimited freedom to explore alternatives, and in far less time.

When the product design is completed and the necessary information is assembled in the computer files, technicians may store the newly developed data, output it on a printer, transfer it to another computer, or send it directly to another step of the automated testing or manufacturing process.

Once the design is approved for production, CAD technicians may use their computers to assist in making detailed drawings of certain parts of the design. They may also prepare designs and drawings of the tools or equipment, such as molds, cutting tools, and jigs, that must be specially made to manufacture the product. As the product moves toward production, technicians, drafters, and designers may work closely with those assembling the product to ensure the same quality found with prototype testing.

CAD technicians must keep records of all of their test procedures and results. They may need to present written reports, tables, or charts to document their test results or other findings. If a particular system, subsystem, or material has not met a testing or production requirement, technicians may be asked to suggest a way to rearrange the system's components or substitute alternate materials.

The company Sutherland works for also uses interoffice and Internet email to communicate with coworkers and the outside world. "I can attach text, a spreadsheet, or a complete three-dimensional CAD model to a message and send it out to several people through a distribution list. It really shortens the cycle of time on a project," he says.

REQUIREMENTS

High School
CAD technicians must be able to read and understand complex engineering diagrams and drawings. The minimum educational requirement for CAD technicians is a high school diploma. If you are a high school student, take courses that provide you with a solid background in algebra, geometry, trigonometry, physics, machine-shop skills, drafting, and electronics, and take whatever computer courses are available. You should also take courses in English, especially those that improve your communications skills.

Postsecondary Training
Increasingly, most prospective CAD technicians are undertaking formal training beyond the high school level, either through a two-year associate's degree program taught at a technical school or community college, or through a four-year college or university program. Employers prefer job applicants who have some form of postsecondary training in drafting.

Such a program should include courses in these areas: basic drafting, machine drawing, architecture, civil drafting (with an emphasis on highways), process piping, electrical, electrical instrumentation, HVAC, and plumbing. There should also be courses in data processing computer programming, systems, and equipment, especially display equipment, computer graphics, product design, and computer peripheral equipment and data storage. Some two-year programs may also require you to complete courses in technical writing, communications, social sciences, and the humanities.

In addition, some companies have their own training programs, which can last as long as two years. Requirements for entry into these company-run training programs vary from company to company.

If you are considering a career in CAD technology, it is important to remember that you will be required to take continuing education courses even after you have found a job. This continuing education is necessary because technicians need to know about recent advances in technology that may affect procedures, equipment, terminology, or programming concepts.

"Technology changes so fast in this area," says Jackie Sutherland of his many years in the drafting and designing field.

Certification or Licensing

Certification for CAD technicians is voluntary. Certification in drafting is available from the American Design Drafting Association. The test, called the Drafter Certification Examination, covers basic drafting skills but does not include testing of CAD drafting. Applicants are tested on geometric construction, architectural terms and regulations, and working sketches.

Licensing requirements vary. Licensing may be required for specific projects, such as a construction project, when the client requires it.

Other Requirements

As a CAD technician or drafter, you will need to think logically, have good analytical skills, and be methodical, accurate, and detail oriented in all your work. You should be able to work as part of a team, as well as independently, since you will spend long periods of time in front of video display screens.

"You have to be able to visualize what a part may look like or what a new version of a part may look like," says Sutherland. "You have to have basic common sense but also be able to look into the future."

EXPLORING

There are a number of ways to gain firsthand knowledge about the field of CAD technology. Unfortunately, part-time or summer jobs involved directly with CAD technology are very hard to find; however, drafting-related jobs can sometimes be found, and many future employers will look favorably on applicants with this kind of experience. In addition, jobs related to other engineering fields, such as electronics or mechanics, may be available and can offer you an opportunity to become familiar with the kind of workplace in which technicians may later be employed.

In addition, high school courses in computers, geometry, physics, mechanical drawing, and shop work will give you a feel for the mental and physical activities associated with CAD technology. Other relevant activities include membership in high school science clubs (especially computer and electronics clubs); participating in science fairs; pursuing hobbies that involve computers, electronics, drafting, mechanical equipment, and model building; and reading books and articles about technical topics.

EMPLOYERS

CAD drafters and technicians are employed in a wide variety of industries, including engineering, architecture, manufacturing, construction, communication, utilities, and the government. They are employed by both large and small companies throughout the United States. For some specialties, jobs may be more specific to certain locations. For example, a drafter or designer for the software industry will find the most opportunities in California's Silicon Valley, while an automotive specialist may be more successful finding jobs near Detroit, Michigan.

STARTING OUT

Probably the most reliable method for entering this field is through your school's career services office. This is especially true for students who graduate from a two-year college or technical institute; recruiters from companies employing CAD technicians sometimes visit such schools, and career services office personnel can help students meet with these recruiters.

As a graduate of a postsecondary program, you can conduct your own job search by contacting architects, building firms, manufacturers, high-technology companies, and government agencies. You can contact prospective employers by phone, email, or with a letter stating your interest in employment, accompanied by a resume that provides details about your education and job experience. State or private employment agencies may also be helpful, and classified ads in newspapers, professional journals, and at association Web sites may provide additional leads.

ADVANCEMENT

CAD technicians who demonstrate their ability to handle more responsibility can expect to receive promotions after just a few years on the job. They may be assigned to design work that requires their special skills or experience, such as troubleshooting problems with systems they have worked with, or they may be promoted to supervisory or training positions. As trainers, they may teach courses at their workplace or at a local school or community college.

In general, as CAD technicians advance, their assignments become less and less routine, until they may have a hand in designing and building equipment. Technicians who continue their education and earn a bachelor's degree may become data processing managers, engineers, or systems analysts or manufacturing analysts.

Other routes for advancement include becoming a sales representative for a design firm or for a company selling computer-aided design services or equipment. It may also be possible to become an independent contractor for companies using or manufacturing CAD equipment.

EARNINGS

Earnings vary among drafters based on the industry they work in as well as their level of experience and the size of their employer. The U.S. Department of Labor reports the median wage for civil and architectural drafters was $43,310 in 2007. The lowest paid 10 percent of these drafters made less than $27,680 annually; the highest paid 10 percent made more than $65,050 annually. Electrical and electronics drafters had somewhat higher earnings, with an average annual wage of $49,250 in 2007. The lowest paid 10 percent of these drafters earned less than $30,490 per year, and the highest paid 10 percent made more than $77,530 yearly.

According to Salary.com, CAD designers/drafters earned salaries that ranged from less than $33,635 to $59,269 or more in 2008.

Actual salaries vary widely depending on geographic location, exact job requirements, and the training needed to obtain those jobs. With increased training and experience, technicians can earn higher salaries, and some technicians with special skills, extensive experience, or added responsibilities may earn more.

Benefits usually include insurance, paid vacations and holidays, pension plans, and sometimes stock purchase plans.

WORK ENVIRONMENT

CAD professionals almost always work in clean, quiet, well-lighted, air-conditioned offices. CAD technicians spend most of their days at a workstation. While the work does not require great physical effort, it does require patience and the ability to maintain concentration and attention for extended periods of time. Some technicians may find they suffer from eyestrain from working for long periods in front of a computer monitor.

CAD technicians, because of their training and experience, are valuable employees. They are called upon to exercise independent judgment and to be responsible for valuable equipment. Out of necessity, they also sometimes find themselves carrying out routine, uncomplicated tasks. CAD technicians must be able to respond well to both kinds of demands. Most CAD technicians work as part of a team. They are required to follow orders, and may encounter situations in which their individual contributions are not fully recognized. Successful CAD technicians are those who work well as team members and who can derive satisfaction from the accomplishments of the team as a whole.

OUTLOOK

The U.S. Department of Labor predicts that employment for drafters will grow more slowly than average for all careers through 2016. The best opportunities will be available to those who have skill and experience using CAD systems. Many companies in the near future will feel pressures to increase productivity in design and manufacturing activities, and CAD technology provides some of the best opportunities to improve that productivity.

Another factor that will create a demand for CAD drafters and technicians is the continued focus on safety and quality throughout manufacturing and industrial fields. To do business or continue to do business with leading manufacturers, companies and lower tier suppliers must meet stringent quality guidelines. With this focus on quality as well as safety, companies are scrutinizing their current designs more carefully than ever, requiring more CAD work for new concepts and alterations that will create a better product.

Any economic downturn could adversely affect CAD technicians because many of the industries that they serve—such as computer and electronics manufacturing, auto manufacturing, or construction—fluctuate greatly with economic swings. In any event, the best opportunities will be for drafters and technicians proficient in CAD technology who continue to learn, both in school and on the job.

Increasing productivity in the industrial design and manufacturing fields will ensure the long-term economic vitality of our nation. CAD technology is one of the most promising developments in this search for increased productivity. Knowing that they are in the forefront of this important and challenging undertaking provides CAD technicians and drafters with a good deal of pride and satisfaction.

FOR MORE INFORMATION

For information about certification, student drafting contests, and job postings, contact
American Design Drafting Association
105 East Main Street
Newbern, TN 38059-1526
Tel: 731-627-0802
http://www.adda.org

For information about the electrical field or to find the IEEE-USA student branch nearest you, contact
Institute of Electrical and Electronics Engineers (IEEE-USA)
2001 L Street, NW, Suite 700
Washington, DC 20036-4910
Tel: 202-785-0017
Email: ieeeusa@ieee.org
http://www.ieeeusa.org

For information about scholarships, grants, and student memberships, contact
Society of Manufacturing Engineers
One SME Drive
Dearborn, MI 48121-2408
Tel: 800-733-4763
http://www.sme.org

Computer and Electronics Sales Representatives

QUICK FACTS

School Subjects
Business
Computer science
Speech

Personal Skills
Communication/ideas
Technical/scientific

Work Environment
Primarily indoors
Primarily multiple locations

Minimum Education Level
Bachelor's degree

Salary Range
$14,780 to $20,150 to
$91,080+

Certification or Licensing
None available

Outlook
About as fast as the average

DOT
275

GOE
10.02.01, 10.03.01

NOC
6421

O*NET-SOC
41-2031.00, 41-4011.03

OVERVIEW

Computer and electronics sales representatives sell hardware, software, peripheral computer equipment, and electronics equipment to customers and businesses of all sizes. Sometimes they follow up sales with installation of systems, maintenance, or training of the client's staff. They are employed in all aspects of businesses. Sales representatives who work for retail stores deal with consumers. Representatives who specialize in a particular piece of hardware, specific software program, or electronic component may do business with banks, insurance companies, or accounting firms, among others.

HISTORY

The first major advances in modern computer technology were made during World War II. After the war, people thought that computers were too big (they easily filled entire warehouses) to ever be used for anything other than government projects, such as their use in compiling the 1950 census.

The introduction of semiconductors to computer technology made smaller and less expensive computers possible. The semiconductors replaced the bigger, slower vacuum tubes of the first computers. These changes made it easier for businesses to adapt computers to their needs, which they began doing as early as 1954. Within 30 years, computers had revolutionized the way people work, play, and even shop. Few occupations have remained untouched by this technological revolution. Consequently, computers are found in businesses, government offices, hospitals, schools, science labs, and homes. Clearly, there is a huge market for the sale of computers and peripheral equipment. There is an important need today for knowledgeable sales representatives to serve both the retail public and to advise corporations and large organizations on their computer and electronics purchases.

THE JOB

The first step in the selling process, whether the sale environment is retail or corporate, is client consultation. Sales representatives determine the client's current technological needs as well as those of the future. During consultation, reps explain the technology's value and how well it will perform. Often, customers do not have expertise in computer or electronics technology, so the rep must explain and translate complicated computer tech-talk as well as answer numerous questions. In retail computer sales, the customer decides what system, peripheral, or software to purchase and then brings it home or arranges for its delivery.

In the corporate sales environment, client consultations usually take longer, often entailing numerous trips to the client's office or place of business. Ron Corrales, an account support manager for Accenture, acknowledges that client consultation is the crucial first step in the sales process. After the client's business is researched and its needs are assessed, possible solutions are outlined in the form of a written or oral presentation. "I was really nervous the first few times I gave a presentation," recalls Corrales. "After all, these were CEOs and CFOs of Fortune 500 companies!" The talent for public speaking and technical writing frequently comes into play. Sales representatives must be able to effectively and clearly present the product and its capabilities, often in layperson's terms. After perfecting his communications skills, Corrales now thinks of client presentations as "just part of the job."

Accenture is one of the largest information technology (IT) consulting firms in the world. It provides proprietary software used by businesses worldwide. Its programs are tools tailor-made to fit the needs of each company and its specific routines, such as accounting, customer billing, inventory control, and marketing, among others. Its client list includes the grocery store chain Kroger's, Harley Davidson, and the U.S. government.

After the presentation, if all goes well, Corrales helps draft the contract. Every aspect of the agreement is outlined and specified—the type of software, length of contract, including services, training, or maintenance. The deal is considered "done" once the Accenture partners and company CEOs sign, and of course, the fees are paid. Once the companies receive their software, it is installed, and glitches, if any, are resolved. Many times company employees are trained by Accenture consultants on how to use the software to its fullest capability. Usually a one-year maintenance contract is provided to the client.

To stay abreast of technological advances, sales representatives must attend training sessions or continuing education classes. It also helps to know the essence of each client's field and the nature of its work. Weekly departmental meetings are necessary to learn of any developments or projects within the department or the company as a whole. A big part of Corrales' job is managing his territory, making client calls or visits when necessary. A chunk of his workday is devoted to "putting out potential client 'fires.'"

REQUIREMENTS

High School
Classes in speech and writing will help you learn how to communicate your product to large groups of people. Computer science and electronics classes will give you a basic overview of the field. General business and math classes will also be helpful.

Postsecondary Training
Though a small number of computer sales positions may be filled by high school graduates, those jobs are scarce. Most large companies prefer a bachelor's or advanced degree in computer or information science, engineering, business, or marketing.

Prepare yourself for a career in this field by developing your computer knowledge. Take computer and math classes, as well as business classes to help develop a sound business sense. Since sales representatives are often required to meet with clients and make sales presentations, excellent communications skills are a must. Hone yours by taking English and speech classes.

In this particular field of sales, extensive computer knowledge is just as important as business savvy. Most computer sales representatives pursue computer science courses concurrently with their business classes. For computer sales representatives specializing in a specific industry (for example, health care or banking), training in the basics and current issues of that field is needed. Such training can be obtained through special work training seminars, adult education classes, or courses at a technical school. Many companies require

A sales representative outlines the features of an Apple iPod for a customer. *(Paul Sakuma, AP Photo)*

their sales staff to complete a training program where they'll learn the technologies and work tools needed for the job. (This is where you'll pick up the techno-speak for your specific field.)

Ron Corrales holds a master of information science degree. One of the college classes that has helped him the most in his career is "technical writing and communication. It helps to be able to explain complicated and technical material in layperson terms."

Other Requirements

As important as having computer and electronics knowledge is having a "sales" personality. Sales representatives must be confident and knowledgeable about themselves as well as the product they are selling. They should have strong interpersonal skills and enjoy dealing with all types of people, from families buying their first PC, to CEOs of a Fortune 500 company. "People in this business are well rounded and enjoy technology," Corrales adds, "but, to do well, they need to be competitively hungry, and like to talk—a lot!"

EMPLOYERS

Employment opportunities for this field exist nationwide. What are your priorities? Do you want to work for an industry giant? IBM? Microsoft? Motorola? You may be enticed with attractive perks, such as stock options, a big travel expense account, or graduate school tuition, among other benefits. Note, however, that these are huge corporations; you'll really have to be something special if you want to stand apart from the other applicants. Getting hired is tough, too. Microsoft, for example, receives thousands of resumes weekly.

Middle-size and small companies usually require their employees to don several hats. That means sales representatives may be responsible for entire presentations, including product and client research, as well as maintenance and service. It may sound like too much work, and for some tasks you may feel overqualified. The rewards include being part of the ground team when your company takes off. If it doesn't, you can always chalk it up to good experience.

STARTING OUT

That Ron Corrales had two job offers by graduation is not uncommon, especially for students with computer-related majors. Many top companies recruit aggressively on campus, often enticing soon-to-be grads with signing bonuses or other incentives at school job fairs.

Other avenues to try when conducting your job search include the newspaper job ads and trade papers. Try the Internet, too. Many companies maintain Web sites where they post employment opportunities as well as receive online resumes and applications. Your school's career services office is a great place to start your job search. Not only will the counselors have information on jobs not advertised in the paper, but they can provide tips on resume writing and interviewing techniques.

ADVANCEMENT

With a good work record, a computer or electronics sales representative may be offered a position in management. A manager is responsible for supervising the sales for a given retail store, sales territory, or corporate branch. A management position comes with not only a higher salary, but a higher level of responsibility as well. An effective manager should be well versed in the company's product and selling techniques and be able to keep a sales group working at top capacity. Those already at the management level may decide to transfer to the marketing side of the business. Positions in marketing may involve planning the marketing strategy for a new computer or electronics product or line, and coordinating sales campaigns and product distribution.

EARNINGS

Because computer and electronics sales reps work in a variety of settings, ranging from the local store on Main Street to large corporations, their annual salaries vary greatly. Sales representatives working in retail are paid an hourly wage, usually minimum wage ($7.25 an hour), which may be supplemented with commissions based on a percentage of sales made that day or week. Salaries are also dependent on the product sold (PCs, mainframes, peripherals) and the market served.

According to the U.S. Department of Labor, earnings for all retail sales reps, including commissions, came to a median of $9.69 per hour in 2007. For full-time work, 40 hours a week, this hourly wage translates into a yearly income of approximately $20,150. At the bottom end of the pay scale were those making less than $7.11 per hour (approximately $14,780 annually), and at the top were those who made more than $18.84 hourly (approximately $39,190 annually). Wholesale and manufacturing sales representatives who specialized in the sale of computer and peripheral equipment had mean annual earnings of $91,080 in 2007.

Computer sales representatives who specialize in corporate sales and installation of hardware or software, like Ron Corrales, tend to earn quite a bit more.

Most computer sales representatives working for large employers are offered a benefits package including health and life insurance, paid holidays and vacations, and continuing education and training, as well as volume bonuses or stock options.

WORK ENVIRONMENT

Retail sales representatives work in a retail environment. A 40-hour workweek is typical, though longer hours may be necessary during busy shopping seasons. Whether the sales representative is compensated during these extended hours varies from store to store. However, increased work times usually means increased sales volume, which in the end translates to more commissions. Retail representatives must be prepared to deal with a large volume of customers with varying levels of technical knowledge, all with many questions. It is necessary to treat customers with respect and patience, regardless of the size of the sale, or when there is no sale at all.

Corporate sales representatives, like Ron Corrales, work in a professional office environment. Work is conducted at the home office as well as in the field when making sales calls. Work schedules vary depending on the size of territory and number of clients. A 40-hour workweek is the exception rather than the rule. "I average about 60-plus hours a week," says Corrales. "My hours are flexible, but with a lot of weekend work and travel."

Also, corporate sales representatives should have excellent communications skills, both in person and on the telephone, because they spend a lot of time consulting with clients. Also, good writing skills are needed when producing proposals and sales reports, often under the pressure of a tight deadline.

OUTLOOK

Employment opportunities for all retail sales representatives are expected to grow about as fast as the average for all careers through 2016, according to the U.S. Department of Labor. Employment growth for those in corporate sales is also expected to grow at this rate.

As computer companies continue to price their products competitively, more and more people will be able to afford new home computer systems or upgrade existing ones with the latest hardware, software, and peripherals. Increased retail sales will increase the need for competent and knowledgeable sales representatives. Many jobs exist at retail giants (Best Buy and Office Depot, known for office-related supplies and equipment, are two examples) that provide consumers with good price packages as well as optional services such as installation and maintenance.

Employment opportunities can also be found with computer specialty stores and consulting companies that deal directly with businesses and their corporate computer and application needs. Computers have become an almost indispensable tool for running a successful business, be it an accounting firm, a public relations company, or a multiphysician medical practice. As long as this trend continues, knowledgeable sales representatives will be needed to bring the latest technological advances in hardware and software to the consumer and corporate level.

All sales workers are adversely affected by economic downturns. In a weak economy, consumers purchase fewer expensive items, and businesses look for ways to trim costs. This results in less of a demand for computers and computer accessories and a reduced need for sales workers.

FOR MORE INFORMATION

For information on internships, student membership, and the student magazine, Crossroads, *contact*
Association for Computing Machinery
2 Penn Plaza, Suite 701

New York, NY 10121-0701
Tel: 800-342-6626
Email: acmhelp@acm.org
http://www.acm.org

For industry and membership information, or for a copy of The
Represento, *a quarterly trade magazine, contact*
Electronics Representatives Association International
300 West Adams Street, Suite 617
Chicago, IL 60606-5109
Tel: 312-527-3050
Email: info@era.org
http://www.era.org

For industry or membership information, contact
North American Retail Dealers Association
222 South Riverside Plaza, Suite 2100
Chicago, IL 60606-6101
Tel: 800-621-0298
Email: nardasvc@narda.com
http://www.narda.com

Computer and Office Machine Service Technicians

QUICK FACTS

School Subjects
Computer science
Technical/shop

Personal Skills
Mechanical/manipulative
Technical/scientific

Work Environment
Primarily indoors
Primarily multiple locations

Minimum Education Level
Associate's degree

Salary Range
$22,640 to $37,100 to
$58,020+

Certification or Licensing
Recommended

Outlook
More slowly than the
average

DOT
633

GOE
05.02.02

NOC
2242

O*NET-SOC
49-2011.00, 49-2011.02,
49-2011.03

OVERVIEW

Computer and office machine service technicians install, calibrate, maintain, troubleshoot, and repair equipment such as computers and their peripherals, office equipment, and specialized electronic equipment used in many factories, hospitals, airplanes, and numerous other businesses. Computer and office machine service technicians, including those who work on automated teller machines, hold approximately 175,000 jobs in the United States.

HISTORY

When computers were first introduced to the business world, businesses found their size to be cumbersome and their capabilities limited. Today, technological advances have made computers smaller yet more powerful in their speed and capabilities. As more businesses rely on computers and other office machines to help manage daily activities, access information, and link offices and resources, the need for experienced professionals to work and service these machines will increase. Service technicians are employed by many corporations, hospitals, and the government, as part of a permanent staff, or they may be contracted to work for other businesses.

THE JOB

L-3 Communications manufactures computer systems for a diverse group of clients such as Shell Oil and United Airlines. Besides computer systems, they also offer services such as equipment maintenance contracts and customer training. Joey Arca, a service technician for L-3 Communications, loves the challenge and diversity of his job. He and other members of the staff are responsible for the installation of computer mainframes and systems, as well as training employees on the equipment. A large part of their work is the maintenance, diagnosis, and repair of computer equipment. Since the clients are located throughout the United States, Arca must often travel to different cities in his assigned district. He also presents company products and services to potential clients and bids for maintenance contracts.

"I don't always have to be at the office, which gives me a lot of freedom," says Arca. "Sometimes I call in from my home and get my scheduled appointments for the day." The freedom of not being deskbound does have its downfalls. "One of the most difficult parts of the job is not knowing when a computer will fail. I carry a pager 24/7, and if I get called, I'm bound to a two-hour response time."

Many times work is scheduled before or after regular working hours or on the weekend, because it's important to have the least amount of workday disruption. Arca is successful in his job because he keeps on top of technology that is constantly changing with continuing education classes and training seminars. He is also well versed in both hardware and software, especially system software.

REQUIREMENTS

High School
Traditional high school courses such as mathematics, physical sciences, and other laboratory-based sciences can provide a strong foundation for understanding basic mechanical and electronics principles. English and speech classes can help boost your written and verbal communications skills. Shop classes dealing with electricity, electronics, and blueprint reading are also beneficial. Computer science classes, of course, will provide you with great experience with computer hardware and software.

Postsecondary Training
You may be able to find work with a high school diploma if you have a lot of practical, hands-on experience in the field. Usually, however, employers require job candidates to have at least an associate's degree in electronics. Joey Arca holds a bachelor of science degree in electrical engineering. He credits specialized classes such as Voice and Data Communications, Microprocessor Controls, and Digital Circuits as giving him a good base for his current work environment.

Certification or Licensing

Most employers require certification, though standards vary depending on the company. However many consider certification as a measure of industry knowledge. Certification can also give you a competitive edge when interviewing for a new job or negotiating for a higher salary.

A variety of certification programs are available from the International Society of Certified Electronics Technicians, the Institute for Certification of Computing Professionals, CompTIA, and Electronics Technicians Association International, among other organizations. After the successful completion of study and examination, you may be certified in fields such as computer, industrial, and electronic equipment. Continuing education credits are required for recertification, usually every two to four years. Arca is certified as a computer technician from the Association of Energy Engineers and the Electronics Technicians Association International.

Other Requirements

A strong technical background and an aptitude for learning about new technologies, good communications skills, and superior manual dexterity will help you succeed in this industry. You'll also need to be motivated to keep up with modern computer and office machine technology. Machines rapidly become obsolete, and so does the service technician's training. When new equipment is installed, service technicians must demonstrate the intellectual agility to learn how to handle problems that might arise.

When asked what kind of people are best suited for this line of work, Arca replies, "Task oriented, quantitatively smart, organized,

Books to Read

Boysen, Earl, and Nancy C. Muir. *Electronics Projects For Dummies*. Hoboken, N.J.: For Dummies, 2006.

Gibilisco, Stan. *Teach Yourself Electricity and Electronics*. 4th ed. New York: McGraw-Hill/TAB Electronics, 2006.

Iovine, John. *Robots, Androids, and Animatrons: 12 Incredible Projects You Can Build*. 2d ed. New York: McGraw-Hill/TAB Electronics, 2001.

McComb, Gordon. *Electronics For Dummies*. 2d ed. Hoboken, N.J.: For Dummies, 2009.

Silver, H. Ward. *Circuitbuilding Do-It-Yourself For Dummies*. Hoboken, N.J.: For Dummies, 2008.

High school students learn how to repair a computer during class. (Bob Daemmrich, The Image Works)

and personable. Also, they need the ability to convey technical terms in writing and orally."

EMPLOYERS

Approximately 175,000 computer and office machine service technicians, including those who work on automated teller machines, are employed in the United States. Potential employers include computer companies and large corporations that need a staff devoted to repairing and maintaining their equipment; electronics, appliance, and office supply stores; electronic and precision equipment repair shops; computer systems design firms; government agencies, and Internet service providers. Many service technicians are employed by companies that contract their services to other businesses. Though work opportunities for service technicians are available nationwide, many jobs are located in large cities where computer companies and larger corporations are based. Approximately 20 percent of computer and office machine service technicians are self employed.

STARTING OUT

If your school offers placement services, take advantage of them. Many times, school placements and counseling centers are privy to job openings that are filled before being advertised in the newspaper.

Make sure your counselors know of any important preferences, such as location, specialization, and other requirements, so they can best match you to an employer. Do not forget to supply them with an updated resume.

There are also other avenues to take when searching for a job in this industry. Many jobs are advertised in the "Jobs" section of your local newspaper. Look under "Computers" or "Electronics." Also, inquire directly with the personnel department of companies that appeal to you and fill out an application. Trade association Web sites are good sources of job leads; many will post employment opportunities as well as allow you to post your resume.

ADVANCEMENT

Due to the growth of computer products and their influence over the business world, this industry offers a variety of advancement opportunities. Service technicians usually start by working on relatively simple maintenance and repair tasks. Over time, they start working on more complicated projects.

Experienced service technicians may advance to positions of increased responsibility, such as a crew supervisor or a departmental manager. Another advancement route is to become a sales representative for a computer manufacturing company. Technicians develop hands-on knowledge of particular machines and are thus often in the best position to advise potential buyers about important purchasing decisions. Some entrepreneurial-minded servicers might open their own repair business, which can be risky but can also provide many rewards. Unless they fill a certain market niche, technicians usually find it necessary to service a wide range of computers and office machines.

EARNINGS

The U.S. Department of Labor reports that the median hourly earnings for computer, automated teller, and office machine technicians were $17.84 in 2007. A technician earning this amount and working full time would have a yearly income of approximately $37,100. The department also reports that the lowest paid 10 percent of all computer and office machine service technicians (regardless of employer) earned less than $10.88 per hour ($22,640 annually). At the other end of the pay scale, 10 percent earned more than $27.90 per hour (approximately $58,020 annually). Those with certification are typically paid more than those without.

Standard work benefits for full-time technicians include health and life insurance and paid vacation and sick time, as well as a retirement plan. Most technicians are given travel stipends; some receive company cars.

WORK ENVIRONMENT

"I like the freedom of not working in a [typical] office environment and the short workweeks," says Joey Arca. Most service technicians, however, have unpredictable work schedules. Some weeks are quiet and may require fewer work hours. However, during a major computer problem, or worse yet, a breakdown, technicians are required to work around the clock to fix the problem as quickly as possible. Technicians spend a considerable amount of time on call, and must carry a pager in case of work emergencies.

Travel is an integral part of the job for many service technicians, many times amounting to 80 percent of the job time. Arca has even traveled to the Philippines, where he worked on the Tomahawk Missile project at Clark Air Force Base. Since he is originally from the Philippines, he was able to combine work with a visit with friends and family.

OUTLOOK

According to the U.S. Department of Labor, employment for service technicians working with computer and office equipment should grow more slowly than the average for all occupations through 2016. Despite this prediction, demand for qualified and skilled technicians will be steady as corporations, the government, hospitals, and universities worldwide continue their reliance on computers to help manage their daily business. Opportunities are expected to be best for those with knowledge of electronics and working in computer repairs. Those working on office equipment, such as digital copiers, should find a demand for their services to repair and maintain increasingly technically sophisticated office machines.

FOR MORE INFORMATION

For information on internships, student membership, and the magazine Crossroads, *contact*

Association for Computing Machinery
2 Penn Plaza, Suite 701
New York, NY 10121-0701
Tel: 800-342-6626
Email: acmhelp@acm.org
http://www.acm.org

For information on certification, contact
Electronics Technicians Association, International
5 Depot Street
Greencastle, IN 46135-8024
Tel: 800-288-3824
Email: eta@eta-i.org
http://www.eta-i.org

For industry and certification information, contact the following organizations:
ACES International
5381 Chatham Lake Drive
Virginia Beach, VA 23464-5400
Tel: 757-499-2850
Email: aces@acesinternational.org
http://www.acesinternational.org

CompTIA
1815 South Meyers Road, Suite 300
Oakbrook Terrace, IL 60181-5228
Tel: 630-678-8300
http://www.comptia.org

Institute for Certification of Computing Professionals
2400 East Devon Avenue, Suite 281
Des Plaines, IL 60018-4619
Tel: 800-843-8227
Email: office@iccp.org
http://www.iccp.org

International Society of Certified Electronics Technicians
3608 Pershing Avenue
Fort Worth, TX 76107-4527
Tel: 800-946-0201, ext. 19
Email: info@iscet.org
http://www.iscet.org

Cost Estimators

OVERVIEW

Cost estimators use standard estimating techniques to calculate the cost of a construction or manufacturing project. They help contractors, owners, and project planners determine how much a project or product will cost to decide if it is economically viable. There are approximately 221,000 cost estimators employed in the United States.

HISTORY

Cost estimators collect and analyze information on various factors influencing costs, such as the labor, materials, and machinery needed for a particular project. Cost estimating became a profession as production techniques became more complex. Weighing the many costs involved in a construction or manufacturing project soon required specialized knowledge beyond the skills and training of the average builder or contractor. Today, cost estimators work in many industries but are predominantly employed in construction and manufacturing.

THE JOB

In the construction industry, the nature of the work is largely determined by the type and size of the project being estimated. For a large building project, for example, the estimator reviews architectural drawings and other bidding documents before any construction begins. The estimator then visits the potential construction site to collect information that may affect the way the structure is built, such as the site's access to transportation, water, electricity, and other needed resources. While out in the field, the estimator also analyzes the topography of the land, taking note of its general characteristics, such

QUICK FACTS

School Subjects
Business
Economics
Mathematics

Personal Skills
Leadership/management
Technical/scientific

Work Environment
Indoors and outdoors
Primarily multiple locations

Minimum Education Level
Some postsecondary training

Salary Range
$32,470 to $54,920 to $91,350+

Certification or Licensing
Recommended

Outlook
Faster than the average

DOT
160

GOE
13.02.04

NOC
2234

O*NET-SOC
13-1051.00

as drainage areas and the location of trees and other vegetation. After compiling thorough research, the estimator writes a quantity survey, or takeoff. This is an itemized report of the quantity of materials and labor a firm will need for the proposed project.

Large projects often require several estimators, all specialists in a given area. For example, one estimator may assess the electrical costs of a project, while another concentrates on the transportation or insurance costs. In this case, it is the responsibility of a *chief estimator* to combine the reports and submit one development proposal.

In manufacturing, estimators work with engineers to review blueprints and other designs. They develop a list of the materials and labor needed for production. Aiming to control costs but maintain quality, estimators must weigh the option of producing parts in-house or purchasing them from other vendors. After this research, they write a report on the overall costs of manufacturing, taking into consideration influences such as improved employee learning curves, material waste, overhead, and the need to correct problems as manufacturing goes along.

To write their reports, estimators must know current prices for labor and materials and other factors that influence costs. They obtain this data through commercial price books, catalogs, and the Internet or by calling vendors directly to obtain quotes.

Estimators should also be able to compute and understand accounting and mathematical formulas to make their cost reports. Computer programs are frequently used to do the routine calculations, producing more accurate results and leaving the estimator with more time to analyze data.

REQUIREMENTS

High School

To prepare for a job in cost estimating, you should take courses in accounting, business, economics, and mathematics. Because a large part of this job involves comparing calculations, it is essential that you are comfortable and confident with your math skills. English courses with a heavy concentration in writing are also recommended to develop your communications skills. Cost estimators must be able to write clear and accurate reports of their analyses. Finally, drafting and shop courses are also useful since estimators must be able to review and understand blueprints and other design plans.

Postsecondary Training

Though not required for the job, most employers of cost estimators in both construction and manufacturing prefer applicants with formal education. In construction, cost estimators generally have associate's or bachelor's degrees in construction management, construction science, or building science. Those employed with manufacturers often have degrees in physical science, business, mathematics, operations research, statistics, engineering, economics, finance, or accounting.

Many colleges and universities offer courses in cost estimating as part of the curriculum for an associate's, bachelor's, or master's degree. These courses cover subjects such as cost estimating, cost control, project planning and management, and computer applications. The Association for the Advancement of Cost Engineering International offers a list of education programs related to cost engineering. Check out the association's Web site, http://www.aacei.org, for more information.

Certification or Licensing

Although it is not required, many cost estimators find it helpful to become certified to improve their standing within the professional community. Obtaining certification proves that the estimator has obtained adequate job training and education. Information on certification procedures is available from organizations such as the American Society of Professional Estimators, the Association for the Advancement of Cost Engineering International, and the Society of Cost Estimating and Analysis.

Other Requirements

To be a cost estimator, you should have sharp mathematical and analytical skills. Cost estimators must work well with others, and be confident and assertive when presenting findings to engineers, business owners, and design professionals. To work as a cost estimator in the construction industry, you will likely need some experience before you start, which can be gained through an internship or cooperative education program.

EXPLORING

Practical work experience is necessary to become a cost estimator. Consider taking a part-time position with a construction crew or manufacturing firm during your summer vacations. Because of more favorable working conditions, construction companies are the busiest during the summer months and may be looking for additional assistance. Join any business or manufacturing clubs that your school may offer.

Another way to discover more about career opportunities is simply by talking to a professional cost estimator. Ask your school counselor to help arrange an interview with an estimator to ask questions about his or her job demands, work environment, and personal opinion of the job.

EMPLOYERS

Approximately 221,000 cost estimators are employed in the United States: 62 percent by the construction industry and 15 percent by manufacturing companies (including those that manufacture electronics and computer products). Other employers include engineering and architecture firms, business services, the government, and a wide range of other industries.

Estimators are employed throughout the country, but the largest concentrations are found in cities or rapidly growing suburban areas. More job opportunities exist in or near large commercial or government centers.

STARTING OUT

Cost estimators often start out working in the industry as laborers, such as construction workers. After gaining experience and taking the necessary training courses, a worker may move into the more specialized role of estimator. Another possible route into cost estimating is through a formal training program, either through a professional organization that sponsors educational programs or through technical schools, community colleges, or universities. School career services counselors can be good sources of employment leads for recent graduates. Applying directly to manufacturers, construction firms, and government agencies is another way to find your first job.

Whether employed in construction or manufacturing, most cost estimators are provided with intensive on-the-job training. Generally, new hires work with experienced estimators to become familiar with the work involved. They develop skills in blueprint reading and learn construction specifications before accompanying estimators to the construction site. In time, new hires learn how to determine quantities and specifications from project designs and report appropriate material and labor costs.

ADVANCEMENT

Promotions for cost estimators are dependent on skill and experience. Advancement usually comes in the form of more responsibility and higher wages. A skilled cost estimator at a large construction company may become a chief estimator. Some experienced cost estimators go into consulting work, offering their services to government, construction, and manufacturing firms.

EARNINGS

Salaries vary according to the size of the construction or manufacturing firm and the experience and education of the worker. According to the U.S. Department of Labor, the median annual salary for cost estimators was $54,920 in 2007. The lowest 10 percent earned less than $32,470 and the highest 10 percent earned more than $91,350. By industry, the mean annual earnings were as follows: nonresidential building construction, $66,470; residential building construction, $58,740; building foundation, structure, and exterior contractors, $58,270; and building finishing contractors, $56,930. Starting salaries for graduates of engineering or construction management programs were higher than those with degrees in other fields. A salary survey by the National Association of Colleges and Employers reports that candidates with degrees in construction science/management were offered average starting salaries of $46,930 a year in 2007.

Benefits for full-time workers include vacation and sick time, health, and sometimes dental, insurance, and pension or 401(k) accounts.

WORK ENVIRONMENT

Much of the cost estimator's work takes place in a typical office setting with access to accounting records and other information. However, estimators must also visit construction sites or manufacturing facilities to inspect production procedures. These sites may be dirty, noisy, and potentially hazardous if the cost estimator is not equipped with proper protective gear such as a hard hat or earplugs. During a site visit, cost estimators consult with engineers, work supervisors, and other professionals involved in the production or manufacturing process.

Estimators usually work a 40-hour week, although longer hours may be required if a project faces a deadline. For construction estimators, overtime hours almost always occur in the summer when most projects are in full force.

OUTLOOK

Employment for cost estimators is expected to increase faster than the average for all occupations through 2016, according to the U.S. Department of Labor. As in most industries, highly trained college graduates and those with the most experience will have the best job prospects.

Many jobs will arise from the need to replace workers leaving the industry, either to retire or change jobs. In addition, growth within the residential and commercial construction industry is a large cause for much of the employment demand for estimators. The fastest growing areas in construction are in special trade and government projects, including the building and repairing of highways, streets, bridges, subway systems, airports, water and sewage systems, and electric power plants and transmission lines. Additionally, opportunities will be good in residential and school construction, as well as in the construction of nursing and extended care facilities. Cost estimators with degrees in construction management, construction science, or building science will have the best employment prospects. In manufacturing, employment is predicted to remain stable, though growth is not expected to be as strong as in construction. Estimators will be in demand because employers will continue to need their services to control operating costs. Estimators with degrees in engineering, statistics, accounting, mathematics, business administration, or economics will have the best employment prospects in this field.

FOR MORE INFORMATION

For information on certification and educational programs, contact
American Society of Professional Estimators
2525 Perimeter Place Drive, Suite 103
Nashville, TN 37214-3674
Tel: 888-EST-MATE
Email: SBO@aspenational.org
http://www.aspenational.org

For information on certification, educational programs, and scholarships, contact
Association for the Advancement of Cost Engineering International
209 Prairie Avenue, Suite 100
Morgantown, WV 26501-5934
Tel: 800-858-2678
Email: info@aacei.org
http://www.aacei.org

For information on certification, job listings, and a glossary of cost-estimating terms, visit the SCEA Web site.
Society of Cost Estimating and Analysis (SCEA)
527 Maple Avenue East, Suite 301
Vienna, VA 22180-4753
Tel: 703-938-5090
Email: scea@sceaonline.net
http://www.sceaonline.net

Electrical and Electronics Engineers

OVERVIEW

Electrical engineers apply their knowledge of the sciences to working with equipment that produces and distributes electricity, such as generators, transmission lines, and transformers. They also design, develop, and manufacture electric motors, electrical machinery, and ignition systems for automobiles, aircraft, and other engines. *Electronics engineers* are more concerned with devices made up of electronic components such as integrated circuits and microprocessors. They design, develop, and manufacture products such as computers, telephones, and radios. Electronics engineering is a subfield of electrical engineering, and both types of engineers are often referred to as electrical engineers. There are approximately 291,000 electrical and electronics engineers employed in the United States.

HISTORY

Electrical and electronics engineering had their true beginnings in the 19th century. In 1800, Alexander Volta made a discovery that opened a door to the science of electricity—he found that electric current could be harnessed and made to flow. By the mid-1800s the basic rules of electricity were established, and the first practical applications appeared. At that time, Michael Faraday discovered the phenomenon of electromagnetic induction. Further discoveries followed. In 1837, Samuel Morse invented the telegraph; in 1876, Alexander Graham Bell invented the telephone; the incandescent

QUICK FACTS

School Subjects
Computer science
Mathematics
Physics

Personal Skills
Mechanical/manipulative
Technical/scientific

Work Environment
Primarily indoors
One location with some
  travel

Minimum Education Level
Bachelor's degree

Salary Range
$51,220 to $81,000 to
  $124,930+

Certification or Licensing
Voluntary

Outlook
Decline

DOT
003

GOE
02.07.04

NOC
2133

O*NET-SOC
17-2071.00, 17-2072.00

lamp (the light bulb) was invented by Thomas Edison in 1878; and the first electric motor was invented by Nikola Tesla in 1888 (Faraday had built a primitive model of one in 1821). These inventions required the further generation and harnessing of electricity, so efforts were concentrated on developing ways to produce more and more power and to create better equipment, such as motors and transformers.

Edison's invention led to a dependence on electricity for lighting our homes, work areas, and streets. He later created the phonograph and other electrical instruments, leading to the establishment of his General Electric Company. One of today's major telephone companies also had its beginnings during this time. Alexander Bell's invention led to the establishment of the Bell Telephone Company, which eventually became American Telephone and Telegraph (AT&T).

The roots of electronics, which is distinguished from the science of electricity by its focus on lower power generation, can also be found in the 19th century. In the late 1800s, current moving through space was observed for the first time; this was called the "Edison effect." In the early 20th century, devices (such as vacuum tubes, which are pieces of metal inside a glass bulb) were invented that could transmit weak electrical signals, leading to the potential transmission of electromagnetic waves for communication, or radio broadcast. The unreliability of vacuum tubes led to the invention of equipment that could pass electricity through solid materials; hence transistors came to be known as solid-state devices.

In the 1960s, transistors were being built on tiny bits of silicon, creating the microchip. The computer industry is a major beneficiary of the creation of these circuits, because vast amounts of information can be stored on just one tiny chip smaller than a dime.

The invention of microchips led to the development of microprocessors. Microprocessors are silicon chips on which the logic and arithmetic functions of a computer are placed. Microprocessors serve as miniature computers and are used in many types of products. The miniaturization of electronic components allowed scientists and engineers to make smaller, lighter computers that could perform the same, or additional, functions of larger computers. They also allowed for the development of many new products. At first they were used primarily in desktop calculators, video games, digital watches, telephones, and microwave ovens. Today, microprocessors are used in electronic controls of automobiles, personal computers, telecommunications systems, and many other products. As a leader in advanced technology, the electronics industry is one of the most important industries today.

THE JOB

Because electrical and electronics engineering is such a diverse field, there are numerous divisions within which engineers work. In fact, the discipline reaches nearly every other field of applied science and technology. In general, electrical and electronics engineers use their knowledge of the sciences in the practical applications of electrical energy. They concern themselves with things as large as atom smashers and as small as microchips. They are involved in the invention, design, construction, and operation of electrical and electronic systems and devices of all kinds.

The work of electrical and electronics engineers touches almost every niche of our lives. Think of the things around you that have been designed, manufactured, maintained, or in any other way affected by electrical energy: the lights in a room, cars on the road, televisions, stereo systems, telephones, your doctor's blood-pressure reader, computers. When you start to think in these terms, you will discover that the electrical engineer has in some way had a hand in science, industry, commerce, entertainment, and even art.

The list of specialties that electrical and electronics engineers are associated with reads like an alphabet of scientific titles—from acoustics, speech, and signal processing; to electromagnetic compatibility; geoscience and remote sensing; lasers and electro-optics; robotics; ultrasonics, ferroelectrics, and frequency control; to vehicular technology. As evident in this selected list, engineers are apt to specialize in what interests them, such as communications, robotics, or automobiles.

As mentioned earlier, electrical engineers focus on high-power generation of electricity and how it is transmitted for use in lighting homes and powering factories. They are also concerned with how equipment is designed and maintained and how communications are transmitted via wire and airwaves. Some are involved in the design and construction of power plants and the manufacture and maintenance of industrial machinery.

Electronics engineers work with smaller-scale applications, such as how computers are wired, how appliances work, or how electrical circuits are used in an endless number of applications. They may specialize in computers, industrial equipment and controls, aerospace equipment, or biomedical equipment.

Tom Busch is an electrical engineer for the U.S. government. He works at the Naval Surface Warfare Center, Crane Division, and much of his work involves testing equipment that will be used on the Navy's ships. "We get equipment that government contractors have put together and test it to make sure it is functioning correctly before it goes out to the fleet," he says. "The type of equipment we test might be anything from navigation to propulsion to communications equipment." Although much of his work currently focuses on testing, Busch also does design work. "We do some software design and also design circuits that go in weapons systems," he says.

Design and testing are only two of several categories in which electrical and electronics engineers may find their niche. Others include research and development, production, field service, sales and marketing, and teaching. In addition, even within each category there are divisions of labor.

Researchers concern themselves mainly with issues that pertain to potential applications. They conduct tests and perform studies to evaluate fundamental problems involving such things as new materials and chemical interactions. Those who work in design and development adapt the researchers' findings to actual practical applications. They devise functioning devices and draw up plans for their efficient production, using computer-aided design and engineering (CAD/CAE) tools. For a typical product such as a television, this phase usually takes up to 18 months to accomplish. For other products, particularly those that utilize developing technology, this phase can take as long as 10 years or more.

Production engineers have perhaps the most hands-on tasks in the field. They are responsible for the organization of the actual manufacture of whatever electric product is being made. They take care of materials and machinery, schedule technicians and assembly workers, and make sure that standards are met and products are quality-controlled. These engineers must have access to the best tools for measurement, materials handling, and processing.

After electrical systems are put in place, *field service engineers* must act as the liaison between the manufacturer or distributor and the client. They ensure the correct installation, operation, and maintenance of systems and products for both industry and individuals. In the sales and marketing divisions, engineers stay abreast of customer needs to evaluate potential applications, and they advise their companies of orders and effective marketing. A *sales engineer* would contact a client interested in, say, a certain type of microchip for its automobile electrical system controls. He or she would learn about the client's needs and report back to the various engineering teams at his or her company. During the manufacture and distribution of the product, the sales engineer would continue to communicate information between company and client until all objectives were met.

All engineers must be taught their skills, and so it is important that some remain involved in academia. *Professors* usually teach a portion of the basic engineering courses as well as classes in the subjects that they specialize in. Conducting personal research is generally an ongoing task for professors in addition to the supervision of student work and student research. A part of the teacher's time is also devoted to providing career and academic guidance to students.

Whatever type of project an engineer works on, he or she is likely to have a certain amount of desk work. Writing status reports and communicating with clients and others who are working on the same project are examples of the paperwork that most engineers are responsible for. Busch says that the amount of time he spends doing desk work varies from project to project. "Right now, I probably spend about half of my time in the lab and half at my desk," he says. "But it varies, really. Sometimes, I'm hardly in the lab at all; other times, I'm hardly at my desk."

REQUIREMENTS

High School

Electrical and electronics engineers must have a solid educational background, and the discipline requires a clear understanding of practical applications. To prepare for college, high school students should take classes in algebra, trigonometry, calculus, biology, physics, chemistry, computer science, word processing, English, and social studies. According to Tom Busch, business classes are also a good idea. "It wouldn't hurt to get some business understanding— and computer skills are tremendously important for engineers, as well," he says. Students who are planning to pursue studies beyond a bachelor of science degree will also need to take a foreign language. It is recommended that students aim for honors-level courses.

Postsecondary Training

Busch's educational background includes a bachelor of science degree in electrical engineering. Other engineers might receive similar degrees in electronics, computer engineering, or another related science. Numerous colleges and universities offer electrical, electronics, and computer engineering programs. Because the programs vary from one school to another, you should explore as many schools as possible to determine which program is most suited to your academic and personal interests and needs. Most engineering programs have strict admission requirements and require students to have excellent academic records and top scores on national college-entrance examinations. Competition can be fierce for some programs, and high school students are encouraged to apply early.

Many students go on to receive a master of science degree in a specialization of their choice. This usually takes an additional two years of study beyond a bachelor's program. Some students pursue a master's degree immediately upon completion of a bachelor's degree. Other students, however, gain work experience first and then take graduate-level courses on a part-time basis while they are employed. A Ph.D. is also available. It generally requires four years of study and research beyond the bachelor's degree and is usually completed by people interested in research or teaching.

By the time you reach college, it is wise to be considering which type of engineering specialty you might be interested in. In addition to the core engineering curriculum (advanced mathematics, physical science, engineering science, mechanical drawing, computer applications), students will begin to choose from the following types of courses: circuits and electronics, signals and systems, digital electronics and computer architecture, electromagnetic waves, systems, and machinery, communications, and statistical mechanics.

Other Requirements

To be a successful electrical or electronics engineer, you should have strong problem-solving abilities, mathematical and scientific aptitudes, and the willingness to learn throughout your career. According to Busch, a curiosity for how things work is also important. "I think you have to like to learn about things," he says. "I also think it helps to be kind of creative, to like to make things."

Most engineers work on teams with other professionals, and the ability to get along with others is essential. In addition, strong communications skills are needed. Engineers need to be able to write reports and give oral presentations.

EXPLORING

People who are interested in the excitement of electricity can tackle experiments such as building a radio or central processing unit of a computer. Special assignments can also be researched and supervised by teachers. Joining a science club, such as the Junior Engineering Technical Society (JETS), can provide hands-on activities and opportunities to explore scientific topics in depth. Student members can join competitions and design structures that exhibit scientific know-how. Reading trade publications, such as the Pre-Engineering Times (http://www.jets.org/newsletter), are other ways to learn about the engineering field. This magazine includes articles on engineering-related careers and club activities.

Students can also learn more about electrical and electronics engineering by attending a summer camp or academic program that focuses on scientific projects as well as recreational activities. For example, summer programs such as the one offered by the Michigan Technological University focus on career exploration in engineering, computers, electronics, and robotics. This academic program for high school students also offers arts guidance, wilderness events, and other recreational activities. (For further information on clubs and programs, contact the sources listed at the end of this article.)

EMPLOYERS

Approximately 291,000 electrical and electronics engineers are employed in the United States. More engineers work in the electrical and electronics field than in any other division of engineering. Most work in engineering and business consulting firms, manufacturing companies that produce electrical and electronic equipment, business machines, computers and data processing companies, and telecommunications parts. Others work for companies that make automotive electronics, scientific equipment, and aircraft parts; consulting firms; public utilities; and government agencies. Some work as private consultants.

STARTING OUT

Many students begin to research companies that they are interested in working for during their last year of college or even before. It is pos-

---

Books to Read

Ashby, Darren. *Electrical Engineering 101: Everything You Should Have Learned in School But Probably Didn't.* New York: Newnes, 2005.

Floyd, Thomas L. *Electronics Fundamentals: Circuits, Devices, and Applications.* 7th ed. Upper Saddle River, N.J.: Prentice Hall, 2006.

Hambley, Allan R. *Electrical Engineering: Principles and Applications.* 4th ed. Upper Saddle River, N.J.: Prentice Hall, 2007.

Peterson's Guides. *Peterson's Graduate Programs in Engineering & Applied Sciences.* 42nd ed. Lawrenceville, N.J.: Peterson's, 2007.

Seifer, Marc J. *Wizard: The Life and Times of Nikola Tesla: Biography of a Genius.* New York: Citadel Press, 2001.

White, Richard, and Roger Doering. *Electrical Engineering Uncovered.* 2d ed. Upper Saddle River, N.J.: Prentice Hall, 2001.

sible to research companies using many resources, such as company directories and annual reports, available at public libraries.

Employment opportunities can be found through a variety of sources. Many engineers are recruited by companies while they are still in college. This is what happened to Tom Busch. "I was interviewed while I was still on campus, and I was hired for the job before I graduated," he says. Other companies have internship, work study, or cooperative education programs from which they hire students who are still in college. Students who have participated in these programs often receive permanent job offers through these companies, or they may obtain useful contacts that can lead to a job interview or offer. Some companies use employment agencies and state employment offices. Companies may also advertise positions through advertisements in newspapers and trade publications. In addition, many newsletters and associations post job listings on the Internet.

Interested applicants can also apply directly to a company they are interested in working for. A letter of interest and resume can be sent to the director of engineering or the head of a specific department. One may also apply to the personnel or human resources departments.

ADVANCEMENT

Engineering careers usually offer many avenues for advancement. An engineer straight out of college will usually take a job as an entry-level engineer and advance to higher positions after acquiring some job experience and technical skills. Engineers with strong technical skills who show leadership ability and good communications skills may move into positions that involve supervising teams of engineers and making sure they are working efficiently. Engineers can advance from these positions to that of a *chief engineer*. The chief engineer usually oversees all projects and has authority over project managers and managing engineers.

Many companies provide structured programs to train new employees and prepare them for advancement. These programs usually rely heavily on formal training opportunities such as in-house development programs and seminars. Some companies also provide special programs through colleges, universities, and outside agencies. Engineers usually advance from junior-level engineering positions to more senior-level positions through a series of positions. Engineers may also specialize in a specific area once they have acquired the necessary experience and skills.

Some engineers move into sales and managerial positions, with some engineers leaving the electronics industry to seek top-level management positions with other types of firms. Other engineers set up their own firms in design or consulting. Engineers can also move into the academic field and become teachers at high schools or universities.

The key to advancing in the electronics field is keeping pace with technological changes, which occur rapidly in this field. Electrical and electronics engineers will need to pursue additional training throughout their careers to stay up-to-date on new technologies and techniques.

EARNINGS

Starting salaries for all engineers are generally much higher than for workers in any other field. Entry-level electrical and electronics engineers with a bachelor's degree earned an average of $55,292, according to a 2007 salary survey by the National Association of Colleges and Employers. Electrical and electronics engineers with a master's degree averaged around $64,416 in their first jobs after graduation, and those with a Ph.D. received average starting offers of $80,206.

The U.S. Department of Labor reports that the median annual salary for electrical engineers was $79,240 in 2007. The lowest paid engineers earned less than $51,220 and the highest paid engineers earned more than $120,650 annually. Electronics engineers earned salaries in 2007 that ranged from less than $53,710 to $124,930 or more, with a median salary of $83,340.

Most companies offer attractive benefits packages, although the actual benefits vary from company to company. Benefits can include any of the following: paid holidays, paid vacations, personal days, sick leave; medical, health, life insurance; short- and long-term disability insurance; profit sharing; 401(k) plans; retirement and pension plans; educational assistance; leave time for educational purposes; and credit unions. Some companies also offer computer purchase assistance plans and discounts on company products.

WORK ENVIRONMENT

Tom Busch's work hours are typically regular—9:00 A.M. to 5:00 P.M., Monday through Friday—although there is occasional overtime. In many parts of the country, this five-day, 40-hour workweek is still the norm, but it is becoming much less common. Many engineers regularly work 10 or 20 hours of overtime a week. Engineers in research and development, or those conducting experiments, often need to work at night or on weekends. Workers who supervise production activities may need to come in during the evenings or on weekends to handle special production requirements. In addition to the time spent on the job, many engineers also participate in professional associations and pursue additional training during their free time. Many high-tech companies allow flex-time, which means that workers can arrange their own schedules within certain time frames.

Most electrical and electronics engineers work in fairly comfortable environments. Engineers involved in research and design may, like Busch, work in specially equipped laboratories. Engineers involved in development and manufacturing work in offices and may spend part of their time in production facilities. Depending on the type of work one does, there may be extensive travel. Engineers involved in field service and sales spend a significant amount of time traveling to see clients. Engineers working for large corporations may travel to other plants and manufacturing companies, both around the country and at foreign locations.

Engineering professors spend part of their time teaching in classrooms, part of it doing research either in labs or libraries, and some of the time still connected with industry.

OUTLOOK

Opportunities for electrical and electronics engineers are expected to increase more slowly than the average for all occupations through 2016, according to the *Occupational Outlook Handbook*. Employment for electrical and electronics engineers in computer and electronic product manufacturing is expected to decline during this same time span. Although demand for electronics should grow, competition from foreign countries and the outsourcing of U.S. engineering jobs to these countries will tend to limit job growth for electrical and electronics engineers in the United States.

The demand for electrical and electronics engineers fluctuates with changes in the economy. In the late 1980s and early 1990s, many companies that produced defense products suffered from cutbacks in defense orders and, as a result, made reductions in their engineering staffs. However, opportunities in defense-related fields have improved, as there is a growing trend toward upgrading existing aircraft and weapons systems. In addition, the increased use of electronic components in automobiles and growth in computer and telecommunications production require a high number of skilled engineers.

The growing consumer, business, and government demand for improved electrical devices (including wireless phone transmitters, electric power generators, high-density batteries, and navigation systems) and electronic goods (including medical electronics, communications equipment, defense-related equipment, and consumer products such as computers and cell phones) is expected to increase demand for engineers. The strongest job growth, however, is likely to be in service-producing industries. This is because more and more firms are contracting for electronic engineering services from consulting and service firms.

Engineers will need to stay on top of changes within the electronics industry and will require additional training throughout their careers to learn new technologies. Economic trends and conditions within the global marketplace have become increasingly more important. In the past, most electronics production was done in the United States or by American-owned companies. During the 1990s, this changed, and the electronics industry entered an era of global production. Worldwide economies and production trends will have a larger impact on U.S. production, and companies that cannot compete technologically may not succeed. Job security is no longer a sure thing, and many engineers can expect to make significant changes in their careers at least once. Engineers who have a strong academic foundation, who have acquired technical knowledge and skills, and who stay up-to-date on changing technologies provide themselves with the versatility and flexibility to succeed within the electronics industry.

FOR MORE INFORMATION

For information on careers and educational programs, contact the following associations:
Institute of Electrical and Electronics Engineers
2001 L Street, NW, Suite 700
Washington, DC 20036-4910
Tel: 202-785-0017
Email: ieeeusa@ieee.org
http://www.ieee.org

Electronic Industries Alliance
2500 Wilson Boulevard
Arlington, VA 22201-3834
Tel: 703-907-7500
http://www.eia.org

For information on careers, educational programs, and student clubs, contact
Junior Engineering Technical Society
1420 King Street, Suite 405
Alexandria, VA 22314-2794
Tel: 703-548-5387

Email: info@jets.org
http://www.jets.org

For information on its summer youth program for high school students, contact
Michigan Technological University Summer Youth Program
Youth Programs Office
1400 Townsend Drive
Houghton, MI 49931-1295
Tel: 906-487-2219
http://youthprograms.mtu.edu

—————— INTERVIEW ——————

Dr. Albert Helfrick is the chair of the Electrical and Systems Engineering Department at Embry-Riddle Aeronautical University in Daytona Beach, Florida. He discussed his career and the education of students with the editors of Careers in Focus: Electronics.

Q. Tell us about your program and your background.

A. The College of Engineering at the Daytona Beach Campus of Embry-Riddle Aeronautical University offers a B.S. in electrical engineering (EE) and degrees in computer engineering and software engineering. The EE degree offers two tracks as well as a nontrack degree. The tracks are avionics and aerospace systems.

My background is in design and management. My degrees are in physics and mathematics and my first job was as a physicist in a research laboratory in high energy physics. I found that the researchers were using my talents for designing their experiments. I became interested in amateur radio when I was 11 years old and have had FCC radio licenses for more than 51 years. My hands-on experience as a novice radio amateur designing and constructing hardware and analyzing problems made me a sought-after young man in the research lab. I also used my commercial radio license to gain employment in radio stations as a broadcast engineer during my college years.

I worked up the corporate ladder to a position of director of engineering for an avionics company but I found the more management I did the less I liked my job, so I resigned my management position and became a full-time consultant and had a small company. My engineers were known for not being afraid to tackle any unusual job. If it involved science and engineering, we would find a solution.

During my entire career I taught college-level classes as an adjunct professor. Seventeen years ago I joined Embry-Riddle to teach full time. The school had an avionics program and they used my textbook—so it was a perfect fit. I am currently the chair of the Electrical and Systems Engineering Department (back to management)

Q. What has been one of your most rewarding career experiences and why?

A. My career is rewarding just about every day. I can't single out only one experience. I have taught literally hundreds of courses over my career, which included not only electrical engineering, but math and physics as well. I teach an avionics short course for the University of Kansas all over the United States and the world. There are many products in use today that I designed or my small consulting firm designed, which is also very rewarding.

There are some experiences that I will always remember; maybe not the most rewarding, but certainly unforgettable such as the time I was invited to testify before Congress. I was asked a question by a Congressman whereupon, being a good professor, I scolded him for not paying attention when I explained the point a few minutes beforehand. Then I realized what I was doing and was very embarrassed.

Q. What are the most important personal and professional qualities for electrical and systems engineers?

A. To be a successful engineer of any discipline you have to love it. I mean you have to eat it, sleep it, dream it—every day. A successful engineering student must be excited by physics, conversant in higher mathematics, and be curious. The engineering student must be a problem solver. The word engineer, which is *ingenieur* in French and German, is related to the words ingenuity and ingenious. Engineers are clever, their designs show originality. The U.S. Patent and Trademark Office only allows ideas that are "novel and not obvious to those of ordinary skill in the art" to be patented. The successful engineer will have these qualities.

Since many engineering designs involve the well-being of humans and the environment not only of the earth but extending into space, engineers must have high standards of ethics.

Engineers are good teachers and communicators. Modern engineering involves large projects where diverse technology is merged into very large and complex systems. Each engineer has a small part in the development of these complex systems and communications in the form of specifications, interface drawings, software, and even audio-visual presentations, and is vital to the success of the project.

Engineers must be good teachers. Once a product is designed, it is turned over to production and finally sold to a customer. The engineers must teach the production department how to make and test the product and instruct the customer how to use the product and the field service organization how to install and repair the product.

Q. What are some typical career paths for graduates of your program?

A. Career paths are many and varied. Since we are aligned with the aerospace industry, most of our students find employment in that field but there are graduates that will be in somewhat related fields.

Electrical and mechanical engineering are the disciplines on which all other engineering is based. More electrical and mechanical engineers are hired than any other. There are very specialized engineers and most undergraduate and high school students don't understand the nature of the highly specialized fields. I advise students to emphasize the fundamentals of mathematics, science, and engineering. Every specialty is based on this foundation. Be a "specialist" in fundamentals. Doing this allows the engineering graduate to go wherever the industry goes.

Q. What advice would you offer students as they graduate and look for jobs?

A. The most important thing when looking for the first job after graduation is to seek out what the student just left—education. By that I mean a job where what the graduate learns on the job will help propel him or her to more challenges and advancement. Also, most companies will pay graduate school tuition, and the new graduate needs to seek and take that opportunity. A bachelor's degree in engineering is not sufficient for a successful career in the 21st century.

Q. What is the employment outlook for the field? Outlook for your program?

A. The future of engineering is always bright as will be the future of our program. Engineers have been around since early man strung rope bridges across streams, the Romans built their aqueducts, mankind electrified the world, and then left the world to explore the moon and planets.

Electricians

OVERVIEW

Electricians design, assemble, install, test, and repair electrical fixtures and wiring. They work on a wide range of electrical and data communications systems that provide light, heat, refrigeration, air-conditioning, power, and the ability to communicate. There are approximately 705,000 electricians working in the United States.

HISTORY

It was during the latter part of the 19th century that electric power entered everyday life. Before then, electricity was the subject of experimentation and theorizing, but had few practical applications. The widespread use of electricity was spurred by a combination of innovations—especially the discovery of a way to transmit power efficiently via overhead lines and the invention of the incandescent lamp, the telephone, and the electric telegraph. In the 1880s, commercial supplies of electricity began to be available in some cities, and within a few years, electric power was transforming many homes and factories.

Today, electricians are responsible for establishing and maintaining vital links between power-generating plants and the many electrical and electronic systems that shape our lives. Along with the electricians who install and repair electrical systems for buildings, the field includes people who work on a wide array of telecommunications equipment, industrial machine-tool controls, marine facilities like ships and offshore drilling rigs, and many other kinds of sophisticated equipment that have been developed using modern technology.

QUICK FACTS

School Subjects
Mathematics
Technical/shop

Personal Skills
Mechanical/manipulative
Technical/scientific

Work Environment
Primarily indoors
Primarily multiple locations

Minimum Education Level
Apprenticeship

Salary Range
$27,330 to $44,780 to
$76,000+

Certification or Licensing
Required by certain states

Outlook
About as fast as the average

DOT
003

GOE
05.02.01, 05.02.02

NOC
2241

O*NET-SOC
47-2111.00

THE JOB

Many electricians specialize in either construction or maintenance work, although some work in both fields. Electricians in construction are usually employed by electrical contractors. Other *construction electricians* work for building contractors or industrial plants, public utilities, state highway commissions, or other large organizations that employ workers directly to build or remodel their properties. A few are self-employed.

When installing electrical systems, electricians may follow blueprints and specifications or they may be told verbally what is needed. They may prepare sketches showing the intended location of wiring and equipment. Once the plan is clear, they measure, cut, assemble, and install plastic-covered wire or electrical conduit, which is a tube or channel through which heavier grades of electrical wire or cable are run. They strip insulation from wires, splice and solder wires together, and tape or cap the ends. They attach cables and wiring to the incoming electrical service and to various fixtures and machines that use electricity. They install switches, circuit breakers, relays, transformers, grounding leads, signal devices, and other electrical components. After the installation is complete, construction electricians test circuits for continuity and safety, adjusting the setup as needed.

Maintenance electricians do many of the same kinds of tasks, but their activities are usually aimed at preventing trouble before it occurs. They periodically inspect equipment and carry out routine service procedures, often according to a predetermined schedule. They repair or replace worn or defective parts and keep management informed about the reliability of the electrical systems. If any breakdowns occur, maintenance electricians return the equipment to full functioning as soon as possible so that the expense and inconvenience are minimal.

Maintenance electricians, also known as *electrical repairers,* may work in large factories, office buildings, small plants, or wherever existing electrical facilities and machinery need regular servicing to keep them in good working order. Many maintenance electricians work in manufacturing industries, such as those that produce automobiles, aircraft, ships, steel, chemicals, and industrial machinery. Some are employed by hospitals, municipalities, housing complexes, or shopping centers to do maintenance, repair, and sometimes installation work. Some work for or operate businesses that contract to repair and update wiring in residences and commercial buildings.

A growing number of electricians are involved in activities other than constructing and maintaining electrical systems in buildings.

An electrician installs a fire alarm and electrical wiring in a condominium.
(Jeff Greenberg, The Image Works)

Many are employed to install computer wiring and equipment, tele-phone wiring, or the coaxial and fiber optics cables used in telecom-munications and computer equipment. Electricians also work in power plants, where electric power is generated; in machine shops, where electric motors are repaired and rebuilt; aboard ships, fixing communications and navigation systems; at locations that need large lighting and power installations, such as airports and mines; and in numerous other settings.

All electricians must work in conformity with the National Electrical Code as well as any current state and local building and electrical codes. (Electrical codes are standards that electrical systems must meet to ensure safe, reliable functioning.) In doing their work, electricians try to use materials efficiently, to plan for future access to the area for service and maintenance on the system, and to avoid hazardous and unsightly wiring arrangements, making their work as neat and orderly as possible.

Electricians use a variety of equipment ranging from simple hand tools such as screwdrivers, pliers, wrenches, and hacksaws to power tools such as drills, hydraulic benders for metal conduit, and electric soldering guns. They also use testing devices such as oscilloscopes, ammeters, and test lamps. Construction electricians often supply their own hand tools. Experienced workers may have hundreds of dollars invested in tools.

REQUIREMENTS

High School

If you are thinking of becoming an electrician, whether you intend to enter an apprenticeship or learn informally on the job, you should have a high school background that includes such courses as applied mathematics and science, shop classes that teach the use of various tools, and mechanical drawing. Electronics courses are especially important if you plan to become a maintenance electrician.

Postsecondary Training

Some electricians still learn their trade the same way electrical workers did many years ago—informally on the job while employed as helpers to skilled workers. Especially if that experience is supplemented with vocational or technical school courses, correspondence courses, or training received in the military, electrical helpers may in time become well-qualified crafts workers in some area of the field.

You should be aware, however, that most professionals believe that apprenticeship programs provide the best all-around training in this trade. Apprenticeships combine a series of planned, structured, supervised job experiences with classroom instruction in related subjects. Many programs are designed to give apprentices a variety of experiences by having them work for several electrical contractors doing different kinds of jobs. Typically, apprenticeships last four to five years and provide at least 144 hours of classroom instruction and 2,000 hours of on-the-job training each year. Completion of an apprenticeship is usually a significant advantage in getting the better jobs in the field.

Applicants for apprenticeships generally need to be high school graduates, at least 18 years of age, in good health, and with at least average physical strength. Although local requirements vary, many applicants are required to take tests to determine their aptitude for the work.

Most apprenticeship programs are developed and conducted by state and national contractor associations such as the Independent Electrical Contractors and the union locals of the International Brotherhood of Electrical Workers. Some programs are conducted as cooperative efforts between these groups and local community colleges and training organizations. In either situation, the apprenticeship program is usually managed by a training committee. An agreement regarding in-class and on-the-job training is usually established between the committee and each apprentice.

Certification or Licensing
Some states and municipalities require that electricians be licensed. To obtain a license, electricians usually must pass a written examination on electrical theory, National Electrical Code requirements, and local building and electrical codes. Electronics specialists receive certification training and testing through the International Society of Certified Electronic Technicians.

Other Requirements
You will need to have good color vision because electricians need to be able to distinguish color-coded wires. Agility and manual dexterity are also desirable characteristics, as are a sense of teamwork, an interest in working outdoors, and a love of working with your hands.

Electricians may or may not belong to a union. While many electricians belong to such organizations as the International Brotherhood of Electrical Workers; the International Union of Electronic, Electrical, Salaried, Machine, and Furniture Workers-Communications Workers of America; the International Association of Machinists and Aerospace Workers; and other unions, an increasing number of electricians are opting to affiliate with independent (nonunion) electrical contractors.

EXPLORING
Hobbies such as repairing radios, building electronics kits, or working with model electric trains will help you understand how electricians work. In addition to sampling related activities like these, you

Mean Annual Earnings for Electricians by Industry, 2007

Natural Gas Distribution	$69,680
Motor Vehicle Manufacturing	$67,060
Performing Arts Companies	$64,040
Motor Vehicle Parts Manufacturing	$63,590
Management of Companies and Enterprises	$62,520
Electric Power Generation, Transmission, and Distribution	$55,910
Local Government	$52,770
Building Equipment Contractors	$47,580
Nonresidential Building Construction	$46,600

Source: U.S. Department of Labor

may benefit by arranging to talk with an electrician about his or her job. With the help of a teacher or guidance counselor, it may be possible to contact a local electrical contracting firm and locate someone willing to give an insider's description of the occupation.

EMPLOYERS

Approximately 705,000 electricians are employed in the United States. Electricians are employed in almost every industry imaginable, from construction (which employs 68 percent of wage and salary workers) to telecommunications to health care to transportation and more. Most work for contractors, but many work for institutional employers that require their own maintenance crews, or for government agencies. Approximately 11 percent of electricians are self-employed.

STARTING OUT

People seeking to enter this field may either begin working as helpers or they may enter an apprenticeship program. Leads for helper jobs may be located by contacting electrical contractors directly or by checking with the local offices of the state employment service or in newspaper classified advertising sections. Students in trade and vocational programs may be able to find job openings through the career services office of their school.

If you are interested in an apprenticeship, you may start by contacting the union local of the International Brotherhood of Electrical Workers, the local chapter of Independent Electrical Contractors, or the local apprenticeship training committee. Information on apprenticeship possibilities also can be obtained through the state employment service.

ADVANCEMENT

The advancement possibilities for skilled, experienced electricians depend partly on their field of activity. Those who work in construction may become supervisors, job site superintendents, or estimators for electrical contractors. Some electricians are able to establish their own contracting businesses, although in many areas contractors must obtain a special license. Another possibility for some electricians is to move, for example, from construction to maintenance work, or into jobs in the shipbuilding, automobile, or aircraft industry.

Many electricians find that after they are working in the field, they still need to take courses to keep abreast of new developments. Unions and employers may sponsor classes introducing new methods and materials or explaining changes in electrical code requirements. By taking skill-improvement courses, electricians may also increase their chances for advancement to better-paying positions.

EARNINGS

Most established, full-time electricians working for contractors average earnings about $21 per hour, or $43,680 per year for full-time work, according to the National Joint Apprenticeship Training Committee—and it is possible to make much more. According to the U.S. Department of Labor, median hourly earnings of electricians were $21.53 in 2007 ($44,780 annually). Wages ranged from less than $13.14 an hour for the lowest paid 10 percent to more than $36.54 an hour for the highest paid 10 percent, or from $27,330 to $76,000 yearly for full-time work. Beginning apprentices earn 40 to 50 percent of the base electrician's wage and receive periodic increases each year of their apprenticeship.

Overall, it's important to realize these wages can vary widely, depending on a number of factors, including geographic location, the industry in which an electrician works, prevailing economic conditions, union membership, and others. Wage rates for many electricians are set by contract agreements between unions and employers. In general, electricians working in cities tend to be better paid than those in other areas. Those working as telecommunications or residential specialists tend to make slightly less than those working as linemen or wiremen.

Electricians who are members of the International Brotherhood of Electrical Workers, the industry's labor union, are entitled to benefits including paid vacation days and holidays, health insurance, pensions to help with retirement savings, supplemental unemployment compensation plans, and so forth.

WORK ENVIRONMENT

Although electricians may work for the same contractor for many years, they work on different projects and at different work sites. In a single year, they may install wiring in a new housing project, rewire a factory, or install computer or telecommunications wiring in an office. Electricians usually work indoors, although some must do tasks outdoors or in buildings that are still under construction. The standard workweek is approximately 40 hours. In many jobs, overtime may be required. Maintenance electricians often have to work some weekend, holiday, or night hours because they must service equipment that operates all the time.

Electricians often spend long periods on their feet, sometimes on ladders or scaffolds or in awkward or uncomfortable places. The work can be strenuous. Electricians may have to put up with noise and dirt on the job. They may risk injuries such as falls off ladders, electrical shocks, and cuts and bruises. By following established safety practices, most of these hazards can be avoided.

OUTLOOK

Employment of electricians will grow about as fast as the average for all occupations through 2016, according to the U.S. Department of Labor. Growth will result from an overall increase in both residential and commercial construction, as well as in power plant construction. In addition, growth will be driven by the ever-expanding use of electrical and electronic devices and equipment. Electricians will be called on to upgrade old wiring and to install and maintain more extensive wiring systems than have been necessary in the past. In particular, the use of sophisticated computer, telecommunications, and data processing equipment and automated manufacturing systems is expected to lead to job opportunities for electricians. Electricians with experience in a wide variety of skills—including voice, data, and video wiring—will have the best employment options.

In addition to opportunities created by growth in the construction and residential industries and other fields, a large number of job openings will occur as a result of workers retiring or leaving the field for other occupations.

While the overall outlook for this occupational field is good, the availability of jobs will vary over time and from place to place. Construction activity fluctuates depending on the state of the local and national economy. Thus, during economic slowdowns, opportunities for construction electricians may not be plentiful. People working in this field need to be prepared for periods of unemployment between construction projects. Openings for apprentices also decline during economic downturns. Maintenance electricians are usually less vulnerable to periodic unemployment because they are more likely to work for one employer that needs electrical services on a steady basis. But if they work in an industry where the economy causes big fluctuations in the level of activity—such as automobile manufacturing, for instance—they may be laid off during recessions.

FOR MORE INFORMATION

For more information about the industry, contact
Independent Electrical Contractors
4401 Ford Avenue, Suite 1100
Alexandria, VA 22302-1432
Tel: 800-456-4324
Email: info@ieci.org
http://www.ieci.org

For information about the rules and benefits of joining a labor union, contact
International Brotherhood of Electrical Workers
900 Seventh Street, NW
Washington, DC 20001-3886
Tel: 202-833-7000
http://www.ibew.org

For information on certification, contact
International Society of Certified Electronic Technicians
3608 Pershing Avenue
Fort Worth, TX 76107-4527
Tel: 800-946-0201
Email: info@iscet.org
http://www.iscet.org

For industry information, contact
National Electrical Contractors Association
3 Bethesda Metro Center, Suite 1100
Bethesda, MD 20814-6302
Tel: 301-657-3110
http://www.necanet.org

For background information on apprenticeship and training programs aimed at union workers, contact
National Joint Apprenticeship and Training Committee
301 Prince George's Boulevard, Suite D
Upper Marlboro, MD 20774-7401
Tel: 301-715-2300
Email: office@njatc.org
http://www.njatc.org

For information on careers, visit
ElectrifyingCareers.com
http://www.electrifyingcareers.com

Electronics Engineering Technicians

OVERVIEW

Electronics engineering technicians work with electronics engineers to design, develop, and manufacture industrial and consumer electronic equipment, including sonar, radar, and navigational equipment, as well as computers, radios, televisions, digital video disc players, stereos, and calculators. They are involved in fabricating, operating, testing, troubleshooting, repairing, and maintaining equipment. Those involved in the development of new electronic equipment help to make changes or modifications in circuitry or other design elements.

Other electronics technicians inspect newly installed equipment or instruct and supervise lower-grade technicians' installation, assembly, or repair activities.

As part of their normal duties, all electronics engineering technicians set up testing equipment, conduct tests, and analyze the results; they also prepare reports, sketches, graphs, and schematic drawings to describe electronics systems and their characteristics. Electronics engineering technicians use a variety of hand and machine tools, including such equipment as bench lathes and drills.

Depending on their specialization, electronics technicians may be computer laboratory technicians, development instrumentation technicians, electronic communications technicians, nuclear reactor electronics technicians, engineering development technicians, or systems testing

QUICK FACTS

School Subjects
Computer science
Mathematics
Physics

Personal Skills
Mechanical/manipulative
Technical/scientific

Work Environment
Primarily indoors
Primarily one location

Minimum Education Level
High school diploma

Salary Range
$31,310 to $52,140 to $75,910+

Certification or Licensing
Voluntary

Outlook
Decline

DOT
003

GOE
02.08.04

NOC
2241

O*NET-SOC
17-3023.00, 17-3023.01

laboratory technicians. There are approximately 170,000 electrical and electronics engineering technicians in the United States.

HISTORY

Strictly speaking, electronics technology deals with the behavior of electrons as they pass through gases, liquids, solids, and vacuums. This field was originally an outgrowth of electrical engineering, an area concerned with the movement of electrons along conductors. As the field of electronics has expanded in scope, however, so has its definition, and today it encompasses all areas of technology concerned with the behavior of electrons in electronic devices and equipment, including electrical engineering.

Although the field of electronics had its most spectacular growth and development during the 20th century, it is actually the product of more than 200 years of study and experiment. One of the important early experimenters in this field was Benjamin Franklin. His experiments with lightning and his theory that electrical charges are present in all matter influenced the thinking and established much of the vocabulary of the researchers who came after him.

The invention of the electric battery, or voltaic pile, by the Italian scientist Alessandro Volta in 1800, ushered in a century of significant discoveries in the field of electricity and magnetism. Researchers working in Europe and the United States made important breakthroughs in how to strengthen, control, and measure the flow of electrons moving through vacuums. In the late 19th and early 20th centuries, these experiments culminated in Sir Joseph John Thomson's description and measurement of the particle now called the electron.

During the early years of the 20th century, further discoveries along these lines were made by experimenters such as Lee De Forest and Vladimir Zworykin. These discoveries led the way to developing equipment and techniques for long-distance broadcasting of radio and television signals. It was the outbreak of World War II, however, with its needs for long-distance communications equipment and, ultimately, missile-guidance systems, that brought about the rapid expansion of electronics technology and the creation of the electronics industry.

As the field of electronics technology turned to the creation of consumer and industrial products following the end of the war, its growth was spurred by two new technological developments. The first was the completion in 1946 of the first all-purpose, all-electronic digital computer. This machine, crude as it was, could handle mathematical calculations a thousand times faster than the electromechanical calculating machines of its day. Since 1946, there has been a steady growth in the speed, sophistication, and versatility of computers.

The second important development was the invention of the transistor in 1948. The transistor provided an inexpensive and compact replacement for the vacuum tubes used in nearly all electronic equipment up until then. Transistors allowed for the miniaturization of electronic circuits and were especially crucial in the development of the computer and in opening new possibilities in industrial automation.

Discoveries during the 1960s in the fields of microcircuitry and integrated circuitry led to the development of more sophisticated microminiaturized electronic equipment, from pocket calculators, digital watches, and microwave ovens to high-speed computers and the long-range guidance systems used in spaceflights.

By the 1970s, electronics had become one of the largest industries and most important areas of technology in the industrialized world, which, in turn, has come to rely on instantaneous worldwide communications, computer-controlled or computer-assisted industrial operations, and the wide-ranging forms of electronic data processing made possible by electronics technology.

Throughout the growth and development of the electronics field, there has been a need for skilled assistants in the laboratory, on the factory floor, and in the wide variety of settings where electronic equipment is used. Electronics engineering technicians fill this important role, and will continue to do so as the electronics industry carries on its rapid growth.

THE JOB

Most electronics technicians work in one of three broad areas of electronics: product development, manufacturing and production, or service and maintenance. Technicians involved with service and maintenance are known as *electronics service technicians*. For information on this area, see the article Electronics Service Technicians.

In the product development area, electronics technicians, or *electronics development technicians,* work directly with engineers or as part of a research team. Engineers draw up blueprints for a new product, and technicians build a prototype according to specifications. Using hand tools and small machine tools, they construct complex parts, components, and subassemblies.

After the prototype is completed, technicians work with engineers to test the product and make necessary modifications. They conduct physical and electrical tests to test the product's performance in various stressful conditions; for example, they test to see how a component will react in extreme heat and cold. Tests are run using complicated instruments and equipment, and detailed, accurate records are kept of the tests performed.

Electronics technicians in the product development field may make suggestions for improvements in the design of a device. They may also have to construct, install, modify, or repair laboratory test equipment.

Electronics drafting is a field of electronics technology closely related to product development. *Electronics drafters,* or *computer-aided design drafters,* convert rough sketches and written or verbal information provided by engineers and scientists into easily understandable schematic, layout, or wiring diagrams to be used in manufacturing the product. These drafters may also prepare a list of components and equipment needed for producing the final product, as well as bills for materials.

Another closely related field is cost estimating. *Cost-estimating technicians* review new product proposals to determine the approximate total cost to produce a product. They estimate the costs for all labor, equipment, and materials needed to manufacture the product. The sales department uses these figures to determine at what price a product can be sold and whether production is economically feasible.

In the manufacturing and production phase, the electronics technicians, who are also called *electronics manufacturing and production technicians,* work in a wide variety of capacities, generally with the day-to-day handling of production problems, schedules, and costs. These technicians deal with any problems arising from the production process. They install, maintain, and repair assembly- or test-line machinery. In quality control, they inspect and test products at various stages in the production process. When a problem is discovered, they are involved in determining the nature and extent of it and in suggesting remedies.

Those involved in quality control inspect and test the products at various stages of completion. They also maintain and calibrate test equipment used in all phases of manufacturing. They determine the causes for rejection of parts or equipment by assembly-line inspectors and then analyze field and manufacturing reports of product failures.

These technicians may make specific recommendations to their supervisors to eliminate the causes of rejects and may even suggest design, manufacturing, and process changes and establish quality-acceptance levels. They may interpret quality control standards to the manufacturing supervisors. And they may establish and maintain quality limits on items purchased from other manufacturers, thus ensuring the quality of parts used in the equipment being assembled.

Another area of electronics technology is that of technical writing and editing. *Technical writers and technical editors* compile, write, and edit a wide variety of technical information. This includes instructional leaflets, operating manuals, books, and installation and service manuals having to do with the products of the company. To do this, they must confer with design and development engineers, production personnel, salespeople, drafters, and others to obtain the necessary information to prepare the text, drawings, diagrams, parts, lists, and illustrations. They must thoroughly understand how and why the equipment works to be able to tell the customer how to use it and the service technician how to install and service it.

At times, technical writers and editors may help prepare technical reports and proposals and write technical articles for engineering societies, management, and other associations. Their job is to produce the means (through printed words and pictures) by which the customer can get the most value out of the purchased equipment. For more information on this career, see the article Technical Writers and Editors.

REQUIREMENTS

High School

A high school diploma is necessary for anyone wishing to pursue a career as an electronics engineering technician. While in high school, you should take algebra, geometry, physics, chemistry, computer science, English, and communications classes. Courses in electronics and introductory electricity are also helpful, as are shop courses and courses in mechanical drawing.

Postsecondary Training

Most employers prefer to hire graduates of two-year postsecondary training programs. These programs provide a solid foundation in the basics of electronics and supply enough general background in science as well as other career-related fields such as business and economics to aid the student in advancing to positions of greater responsibility.

Two-year associate-degree programs in electronics technology are available at community colleges and technical institutes. Programs vary quite a bit, but in general, a typical first-year curriculum includes courses in physics for electronics, technical mathematics, communications, AC/DC circuit analysis, electronic amplifiers, transistors, and instruments and measurements.

Typical second-year courses include physics, applied electronics, computer information systems, electronic drafting, electronic instruments and measurements, communications circuits and systems, digital electronics, technical writing, and control circuits and systems.

Students unable to attend a technical institute or community college should not overlook opportunities provided by the military. The military provides extensive training in electronics and other related fields. In addition, some major companies, particularly utilities, hire people straight out of high school and train them through in-house programs. Other companies promote people to technicians' positions from lower-level positions, provided they attend educational workshops and classes sponsored by the company.

Certification or Licensing

Electronics engineering technicians may obtain voluntary certification from the International Society of Certified Electronics Technicians and the Electronics Technicians Association, International. This certification is regarded as a demonstration of professional dedication, determination, and expertise.

Other Requirements

You should have an interest in and an aptitude for mathematics and science and should enjoy using tools and scientific equipment. On the personal side, you should be patient, methodical, persistent, and able to get along with different kinds of people. Because technology changes so rapidly, you will need to pursue additional training throughout your career. To work in electronics engineering, you also need to have the ability and desire to learn quickly, an inquisitive mind, and the willingness to read and study materials to keep up to date.

EXPLORING

If you are interested in a career as an electronics engineering technician, you can gain relevant experience by taking shop courses, joining electronics or radio clubs in school, and assembling electronic equipment with commercial kits.

You should take every opportunity to discuss the field with people working in it. Try to visit a variety of different kinds of electronics facilities—service shops, manufacturing plants, and research laboratories—either through individual visits or through field trips organized by teachers or guidance counselors. These visits will provide a realistic idea of the opportunities in the different areas of the electronics industry. You should also take an introductory course in electricity or electronics to test your aptitude, skills, and interest. If you enroll in a community college or technical school, you may

Did You Know?

Approximately 1.3 million wage and salary workers were employed in the computer and electronic product manufacturing industry in 2006. Workers were employed in the following specialty segments:

Manufacturing Industry Segment Segment Employed	Percentage of Workers
Semiconductor and Other Electronic Components	35.2 percent
Navigational, Measuring, Electromedical, and Control Instruments	33.3 percent
Computer and Peripheral Equipment	15.1 percent
Communications Equipment	10.9 percent
Magnetic and Optical Media	3.1 percent
Audio and Visual Equipment	2.4 percent

Source: U.S. Department of Labor

be able to secure off-quarter or part-time internships with local employers through your school's career services office. Internships are valuable ways to gain experience while still in school.

EMPLOYERS

Approximately 170,000 electrical and electronics engineering technicians are employed in the United States. Electronics engineering technicians are employed by companies that design, develop, and manufacture industrial and consumer electronic equipment. Such employers include service shops, manufacturing plants, and research laboratories.

STARTING OUT

You may be able to find your first full-time position through your school's career services office. These offices tend to develop very good working relationships with area employers and can offer you excellent interviewing opportunities.

Another way to obtain employment is through direct contact with a particular company. It is best to write to the personnel department and include a resume summarizing your education and experience. If the company has an appropriate opening, a company representative will schedule an interview with you. There are also many excellent public and commercial employment organizations that can help graduates obtain jobs appropriate to their training and experience. In addition, the classified ads in most metropolitan Sunday newspapers list a number of job openings with companies in the area.

Professional associations compile information on job openings and publish job lists. For example, the International Society of Certified Electronics Technicians offers lists of job openings at its Web site. Information about job openings can also be found in trade magazines on electronics.

ADVANCEMENT

Advancement possibilities in the field of electronics are almost unlimited. Technicians usually begin work under the direct and constant supervision of an experienced technician, scientist, or engineer. As they gain experience or additional education, they are given more responsible assignments, often carrying out particular work programs under only very general supervision. From there, technicians may move into supervisory positions; those with exceptional ability can sometimes qualify for professional positions after receiving additional academic training.

The following paragraphs briefly describe some of the positions to which electronics technicians can advance.

Electronics technician supervisors work on more complex projects than do electronics technicians. They supervise other technicians and may also have administrative duties, such as making the employee work schedule, assigning laboratory projects to various technicians, overseeing the training progress of new employees, and keeping the workplace clean, organized, and well stocked. In general, they tend to have more direct contact with project managers and project engineers.

Engineering technicians are senior technicians or engineering assistants who work as part of a team of engineers and technicians in research and development of new products. Additional education, resulting in a bachelor of science degree in engineering, is required for this position.

Production test supervisors make detailed analyses of production assembly lines to determine where production tests should be placed along the line and the nature and goal of the tests. They may be responsible for designing the equipment setup used in production testing.

Quality control supervisors determine the scope of a product sampling and the kinds of tests to be run on production units. They translate specifications into testing procedures.

Workers who want to advance to engineering positions can become electrical engineers or electronics engineers through additional education. A bachelor of science degree in engineering is required.

All electronics technicians will need to pursue additional training throughout their careers to keep up-to-date with new technologies and techniques. Many employers offer continuing education in the form of in-house workshops or outside seminars. Professional associations also offer seminars and classes on newer technologies and skill building.

EARNINGS

The U.S. Department of Labor reports that in 2007, median annual earnings for electrical and electronics engineering technicians were $52,140. Salaries ranged from less than $31,310 for the lowest paid 10 percent to more than $75,910 for the highest paid 10 percent.

Electronics engineering technicians generally receive premium pay for overtime work on Sundays and holidays and for evening and night-shift work. Most employers offer benefits packages that include paid holidays, paid vacations, sick days, and health insurance. Companies may also offer pension and retirement plans, profit sharing, 401(k) plans, tuition assistance programs, and release time for additional education.

WORK ENVIRONMENT

Because electronic equipment usually must be manufactured in a dust-free, climate-controlled environment, electronics engineering technicians can expect to work in modern, comfortable, well-lighted surroundings. Many electronics plants have been built in industrial parks with ample parking and little traffic congestion. Technicians who work with cable, Master Antenna Television, satellites, and antennas work outside. Frequency of injuries in the electronics industry is far less than in most other industries, and injuries that do occur are usually not serious.

Most employees work a 40-hour workweek, although overtime is not unusual. Some technicians regularly average 50 to 60 hours a week.

OUTLOOK

The electronics industry is expected to remain one of the most important industries in the United States through the next decade. Consumer products such as large screen and high-definition televisions, MP3 players, cellular phones, digital video disc recorders, compact disc players, personal computers and related hardware, and home appliances with solid-state controls are constantly evolving and in high demand. Two areas showing high growth are computers and tele-communications products. Multimedia and interactive products are expanding rapidly, and many new products are expected in the coming years. In addition, increasing automation and computer-assisted manufacturing processes rely on advanced electronic technology.

Despite this prediction, the U.S. Department of Labor estimates that opportunities for electronics engineering technicians will grow more slowly than the average for all occupations through 2016. Employment for electronics engineering technicians in computer and electronic product manufacturing is expected to decline during this same time span. Foreign design and manufacturing competition and general economic conditions will limit growth for electronics engineering technicians.

Prospective electronics technicians should begin paying attention to certain factors that might affect the areas in which they are thinking of working. For example, electronics technicians planning to work for the military or for a military contractor or subcontractor in radar technology need to keep an eye on federal legislation concerning military spending cuts or increases.

The electronics industry is undeniably indispensable to our lives, and although there will be fluctuations in growth for certain sub-fields, there will be a need for qualified personnel in others. The key to success for an electronics technician is to stay up to date with technology and to be professionally versatile. Building a career on a solid academic foundation and hands-on experience with basic electronics enables an electronics technician to remain competitive in the job market.

FOR MORE INFORMATION

For industry information and to subscribe to Certified Engineering Technician (CET) *magazine, contact*
American Society of Certified Engineering Technicians
PO Box 1536
Brandon, MS 39043-1536
Tel: 601-824-8991
http://www.ascet.org

For industry information, contact
Electronic Industries Alliance
2500 Wilson Boulevard
Arlington, VA 22201-3834
Tel: 703-907-7500
http://www.eia.org

For information on certification, contact
Electronics Technicians Association, International
5 Depot Street
Greencastle, IN 46135-8024
Tel: 800-288-3824
Email: eta@eta-i.org
http://www.eta-sda.com

For information on careers in electrical and electronics engineering, contact
Institute of Electrical and Electronics Engineers
2001 L Street, NW, Suite 700
Washington, DC 20036-4910
Tel: 202-785-0017
Email: ieeeusa@ieee.org
http://www.ieeeusa.org

For information on certification, contact
International Society of Certified Electronics Technicians
3608 Pershing Avenue
Fort Worth, TX 76107-4527
Tel: 817-921-9101
Email: info@iscet.org
http://www.iscet.org

Visit the JETS Web site to read the online brochure Engineering Technologists and Technicians.
Junior Engineering Technical Society (JETS)
1420 King Street, Suite 405
Alexandria, VA 22314-2794
Tel: 703-548-5387
Email: info@jets.org
http://www.jets.org

Electronics Service Technicians

QUICK FACTS

School Subjects
Mathematics
Physics

Personal Skills
Mechanical/manipulative
Technical/scientific

Work Environment
Primarily indoors
Primarily multiple locations

Minimum Education Level
Associate's degree

Salary Range
$20,640 to $31,260 to
$49,130+

Certification or Licensing
Voluntary (certification)
Required by certain states
(licensing)

Outlook
More slowly than the average

DOT
828

GOE
05.02.02

NOC
2242

O*NET-SOC
49-2097.00

OVERVIEW

Electronics service technicians work with and repair consumer electronic equipment that is malfunctioning. This equipment typically includes televisions, audio and video equipment, computers, microwave ovens, and other kinds of home electronic devices. Service technicians diagnose problems in the equipment and make the repairs necessary to restore the equipment to working order. Technicians may also advise customers on the equipment's replacement when it is no longer practical to maintain. Some electronics service technicians may work with electronic office equipment, such as photocopy machines, dictating machines, and fax (facsimile) machines. There are about 40,000 electronic home entertainment equipment installers and repairers working in the United States.

HISTORY

Most electronic products in use today were developed during the 20th century; however, they are based on principles of electronics discovered in the 19th century. Modern television, for instance, is based on principles first demonstrated in the 1850s by Heinrich Geissler, whose experiments showed that electricity discharged in a vacuum tube caused small amounts of rare gases in the tube to glow. Later investigations showed that the glow was caused by the freeing of electrons. Experimenters in the late 1800s and early 1900s further refined the vacuum tube. Then, in 1898, Karl Braun made the first cathode ray tube that could control the electron flow. In 1907,

Lee De Forest developed the first amplifying tube, used to strengthen electronic signals.

At this point, the basic elements of modern television transmission existed, but they had not yet been combined into a workable system. In 1922, a 16-year-old named Philo Farnsworth developed a practical electronic scanning system. Shortly afterwards, in 1923, Vladimir Zworykin developed the iconoscope and the kinescope, which were, respectively, the basic elements of the television camera and the television receiver. Zworykin's first practical all-electronic television system was demonstrated for the first time publicly in 1929.

Radio followed a similar path of development. But, although the roots of television and radio lie in the 1800s, neither medium had developed to the point of needing a service industry until regular commercial broadcasting began and people began to purchase receivers. For radio, commercial broadcasting began in 1920, when KDKA, Pittsburgh, and WWWJ, Detroit, went on the air. For television, regular broadcasting began with six stations, which went on the air in 1946. Just four years later in 1950, there were six million television sets in the United States. In 2007, there were an estimated 111.4 million TV households in the United States.

Owners of the early radios handled most of their own repairs; sets were simple, and the range of possible solutions to problems was small. As the broadcasting industry grew and new improvements resulted in more complicated sets, trade and technical institutes were established to train technicians. Correspondence schools started and became popular during the Great Depression of the 1930s, when many people were seeking new careers or ways to supplement their incomes.

The explosive growth of television broadcasting after World War II created an almost instant demand for trained television service technicians. Trade and technical schools again boomed, aided this time by the GI Bill's educational benefits, which enabled many veterans to study television servicing. The field was especially attractive to former servicemen who had been communications or electronics technicians in the U.S. armed forces. The subsequent development of the transistor, stereophonic sound, and color television resulted in television sets, radios, and other home electronics equipment that could only be serviced by trained technicians with adequate testing equipment and repair tools.

The development of the microchip in the late 1960s led to the invention of many new electronic products. Tremendous growth occurred in the 1970s and 1980s in the number and variety of electronic devices introduced into homes and businesses. Miniature and large screen projection televisions, video cameras and videocassette recorders (VCRs), microcomputers and printers, microwave ovens, and telephone answering machines all became common household items. Fax machines, desktop photocopiers, and electronic securities systems became common in offices.

In the 1990s, advances in microprocessors—tiny computer chips that contain all of the operating functions of a computer—led to a vast array of electronic products available to consumers both in offices and homes. Today, many homes have personal computers, compact disc players, fax machines, mobile phones, and advanced home security systems. New products, such as interactive and high-definition televisions, multimedia computers, electronic image scanning equipment, DVD players, and sophisticated telecommunications products are being developed along with many other electronic products. The growth in this field has led to a continuing need for trained technicians to maintain and repair the many types of home and office electronics equipment.

THE JOB

James McNees is a service operations manager for H. H. Gregg Appliances. His job is to service and repair consumer electronics products. He services home entertainment equipment such as television sets, videocassette recorders, compact disc players, radios, and audio recording equipment. McNees also services electronic equipment such as garage door openers, microwave ovens, and kitchen appliances. Although McNees does not work on personal computers and peripheral equipment, some electronics service technicians do. They may also service home security systems, antennas, satellite reception equipment, electronic organs, and amplifying equipment for other electrified musical instruments.

Technicians may service equipment that is working properly. They also diagnose and repair malfunctioning equipment. They usually begin by gathering information from customers about the problems they are having with their equipment. Because today's consumer electronics are so sophisticated, often the consumer simply does not know how to operate the machine, according to McNees. After talking with the customer, the technician makes a preliminary inspection of the equipment. This inspection may reveal a loose connection or other simple problem, and the technician may be able to complete repairs quickly. In other cases, a problem may be more complicated and may require that the equipment be taken to a shop for more thorough testing and the installation of new components.

Electronics service technicians are classified as *inside* or *outside technicians,* although some work as both inside and outside technicians. Outside, or *field,* technicians make service calls on customers, gather information, and make preliminary examinations of malfunctioning equipment. They may also install new equipment. "When a tech is working in the field, he does the diagnostics at a more surface level," McNees says. "They are limited on time because they might have eight to 10 houses to visit, so if a field tech doesn't know what the problem is within 20 minutes, he'll probably have to bring it [the equipment] in."

As an inside technician, McNees works in a shop, where he makes more thorough examinations of problems using testing equipment and hand tools such as pliers and socket wrenches to dismantle sets and make repairs. He uses testing equipment such as voltage meters, oscilloscopes, signal generators, monitor testers, analyzers, and frequency counters.

Some of the tasks that both inside and outside technicians perform include reading service manuals and wiring diagrams, operating testing equipment, replacing defective parts, installing solid-state electronic components, making adjustments in electronic controls, cutting and connecting wires, and soldering metal components together. Technicians also write reports about the service or repairs done and calculate bills for parts and labor costs.

The servicing of other kinds of electronic equipment, such as audio and digital video disc recorders, requires special knowledge of their components. Electronics technicians learn about such special areas and keep up with new developments in electronics by attending short courses given by manufacturers at their factories, by factory technicians at local shops, or through professional associations.

Another area of specialization is computer service and repair. *Computer service technicians* specialize in installing, servicing, and repairing computers and related equipment such as printers. They need to be familiar with the many components and assemblies making up a computer and be able to advise people on the necessary equipment needed to upgrade systems. They may also advise consumers on compatible equipment they can add to their existing equipment to allow new functions, such as modems that connect computers to telephone lines and allow the use of fax machines and Internet access. For more information on this career, see the article Computer and Office Machine Service Technicians.

REQUIREMENTS
High School
If you are considering a career as an electronics service technician, you can begin preparing while still in high school by taking as

many science and mathematics courses as possible. At minimum, you should take algebra, geometry, physics, and chemistry. Other useful classes are English, communications, applied mathematics, and shop classes. Shop classes that teach the basics of electricity and the use of hand tools and provide an introduction to electronic measurement devices and testing equipment are especially helpful. English and communications classes help provide you with the language skills you will need to read electronics texts and manuals comfortably and to express yourself well when making spoken and written proposals.

Postsecondary Training

Most of the service technicians in James McNees's company have at least an associate's degree in electronic technology. These degrees can typically be obtained at either a technical institute or community college. Community colleges and technical schools offer both one- and two-year programs that provide more extensive training in electronics. One-year programs concentrate on electronics and related courses and result in certification in a specific area of study. Two-year programs include electronics courses and other more in-depth courses that result in an associate's degree. Most employers, like McNees's employer, prefer to hire graduates of two-year programs.

In addition to electronic technology, community colleges and technical schools may offer other, similar programs such as electronics and electrical/electronics technology. These programs are usually broad-based electronics programs geared to electronics technicians in general, rather than specifically to service technicians.

Students enrolled in a one-year program may take classes such as electronic assembly techniques, electronic circuits, and technical mathematics. Students in two-year programs will study those topics, as well as physics, computer information systems, electronic drafting, microprocessors, digital electronics, applied electronics, electronic instruments and measurements, and communication electronics. Many students also take technical writing. Other classes may focus on specific types of repairs, such as servicing computer monitors or video laser discs.

Students who are unable to attend a vocational school or technical institute may wish to consider opportunities provided by the military. The military offers extensive training in electronics to members of the armed forces and provides valuable practical experience. Visit Today's Military (http://www.todaysmilitary.com) for more information.

In some cases, workers learn through an apprenticeship program, which combines on-the-job training with classroom instruction. This is not as common for electronics service technicians, however, as for other types of electronics technicians. Apprenticeships generally last four years.

Extensive on-the-job training is becoming much less common. Whereas shops formerly provided complete on-the-job instruction for untrained employees, they now usually limit such training to current employees—delivery drivers, antenna installers, and so forth—who show a basic understanding of electronics, an aptitude for careful work, and an interest in learning. Such opportunities usually occur in shops that place a higher value on practical experience than on theory. Even so, individuals in such programs will have to supplement their practical training with evening school or home study courses.

Certification or Licensing

Certain states require some electronics sales and service technicians to be licensed. Such licenses are obtained by passing tests in electronics and demonstrating proficiency with testing equipment. Prospective technicians should check with a training institution in their state to determine whether licensing is required. Some workers in this field also opt to take a voluntary certification examination. Several certifications are offered by the International Society of Certified Electronic Technicians and the Electronics Technicians Association, International. Contact these organizations for more information.

Other Requirements

To be a successful electronics service technician, you should have mathematical aptitude, problem-solving capability, the ability to learn quickly, and the willingness to learn throughout your career. A solid mechanical aptitude and knowledge of practical electronics are also vital. You should be familiar with and able to use electrical hand tools and basic electronic and electrical testing equipment. Because precision and accuracy are often required in adjusting electronic equipment, you should be detail oriented, according to McNees.

Technicians also need good interpersonal and communications skills since this type of work involves interacting with a wide variety of people. These technicians often work in customers' homes and should be able to meet and communicate clearly with strangers. The ability to extract useful information from customers about their equipment can be a great time-saver.

Because of the constantly changing technology of electronic devices, electronics service technicians must be willing to keep growing and learning in their trade if they are to be successful. This may require going back to school to learn new technologies and equipment or taking classes through professional associations.

Technicians who work in the field or as outside technicians need a driver's license and a good driving record. In most cases, employers provide a vehicle to drive to customers' homes and businesses, but some shops may require a technician to provide his or her own vehicle.

EXPLORING

If you are interested in the electronics field, you have many opportunities to explore your interests and aptitudes for this type of work. Joining a science or electronics club and participating in competitions provide hands-on activities and experiences related to different facets of electronics. You might also build electronic kits, take apart radios and television sets (be sure to work with an experienced electronics service technician when trying this), or test your repair abilities on discarded appliances. Reading electronics magazines is another way to explore the wide field of electronics and learn about specific types of technology, such as digital and telecommunications technologies.

Another way to learn about the actual work electronics service technicians do is to talk with people in the field. Local electronics service technicians are usually willing to share their experience and knowledge with interested young people. Owners of stores or repair shops may be especially helpful with the business aspects of a career in this field. Summer employment as a helper or a delivery person can provide an opportunity to observe the day-to-day activities of technicians.

You can also request information from schools that offer training in electronics and other related fields to find out what kind of programs are available. Local chapters of the International Brotherhood of Electrical Workers and local offices of the state employment service can also supply information about training opportunities as well as the employment outlook in a specific area.

EMPLOYERS

Approximately 40,000 electronic home entertainment equipment installers and repairers are employed in the United States. Electronics service technicians who specialize in servicing home entertainment equipment usually work in electronics service centers, in stores that sell home entertainment equipment, or in electronics repair shops. There are several medium-sized to large chains of electronics superstores scattered throughout the United States. One of the largest chains is Best Buy. Most of these types of chain stores employ technicians in their service departments. There are also many small, independently owned electronics repair shops, found in virtually every city. The best way to locate these small independent shops is to check the area's Yellow Pages under Electronic Equipment, Electronics Service, or Electronics Repair.

STARTING OUT

Most people enter this field after completing some type of formal training program in a technical school or community college. Employers generally prefer to hire graduates of two-year programs in electronics or a related field. Students who are enrolled in a community college or technical institute may learn about job openings through their schools' career services office. They may also find out about job openings or prospective employers through contacts they make during training and through teachers and school administrators.

Applicants may also apply directly to a company that hires electronics service technicians, such as a service department of a large retail firm, a specialty shop that sells and repairs electronic equipment, or a shop that specializes in electronics repairs. Most companies provide some sort of on-the-job training, either through classes in repair techniques or by assigning new employees to work with an experienced worker who trains them and supervises their work. In some cases, especially for workers who have not completed technical training, new employees require a year of shop supervision before they are able to work independently without the direction of a more experienced electronics technician.

ADVANCEMENT

Advancement in this field depends to a large extent on the size and character of the technician's place of employment. Early advancement usually comes in the form of increased salary and less supervision in recognition of the technician's increasing skill. For a technician who works in a small shop, the only other advancement possibility may be going into business on his or her own, if the community can support another retail store or repair shop.

Persons interested in working for themselves often open up their own shops or work as freelance technicians. Freelance technicians usually operate out of their homes and perform the same services as other technicians.

In a larger store or shop, the electronics technician usually advances to a supervisory position, such as *crew chief, sales supervisor, senior technician,* or *service* or *sales manager.* This may involve not only scheduling and assigning work, but also training new employees and arranging refresher courses and factory training in new products for experienced electronics technicians.

Technicians with strong theoretical training in electronics may go on to become technical school instructors. They may also become service representatives for manufacturers. Those employed in stores or shops that handle a wide variety of electronics sales and service work may become involved in working on more complicated equipment, from radio-frequency heating equipment to electron microscopes and computer systems. This expertise may also lead to working with engineers in designing and testing new electronic equipment.

Because the work that electronics service technicians do is similar to that done by industrial electronics technicians, some technicians transfer to the industrial electronics segment. Technicians may also become electrical or electronics engineers through additional education resulting in a bachelor of science degree in engineering.

EARNINGS

The median hourly wage of full-time electronics service technicians was $15.03 in 2007, according to the U.S. Department of Labor. Based on a 40-hour workweek, this works out to approximately $31,260 annually. Workers at the lowest 10 percent end of the scale earned less than $9.92—or roughly $20,640 annually. The highest paid 10 percent of electronics service technicians earned more than $23.62 hourly—or about $49,130 annually. Benefits vary depending on the type and size of employer, geographic location, and type of work done. Companies may offer any of the following benefits: paid vacations, paid holidays, health insurance, life insurance, retirement plans, educational assistance, 401(k) plans, and profit sharing.

WORK ENVIRONMENT

Most electronics service technicians work a standard 40-hour week, Monday through Friday. Their work is usually performed indoors, in homes and shops, under generally comfortable conditions. Technicians working on cable and satellite equipment work outdoors. Actual working conditions vary based on the type of company a technician works for. A large retail store may have a lot more activity, noise, and customer contact than a quiet electronics repair shop that has few visitors. Technicians who work in specialty stores, such as musical equipment retailers, may work in noisy surroundings, with many types of music playing at the same time.

Outside technicians may spend considerable time driving from call to call. Their work may take them to a variety of neighborhoods, and they need to feel comfortable with people from varying backgrounds. "A big part of the field technician's job is customer relations," says James McNees.

All technicians risk occasional electrical shock, but this risk is minimized greatly by following proper safety precautions. Their work may involve lifting heavy items, working with delicate parts, and working in tight spaces. Depending on the type of repair, bending and stretching may be required.

Once they have completed their training, electronics service technicians work with a minimum of supervision. They must, however, be able to work carefully and accurately. Because the result of their work is often immediately evident to the owner of the equipment, service technicians must be able to handle criticism when they are not completely successful.

Self-employed technicians may operate out of their homes, where they keep a shop in the basement, garage, or a special workroom. Others operate small shops and hire workers to help run the shop or assist in repairs.

OUTLOOK

Even though the demand for and use of consumer electronics equipment is expected to increase, employment of electronics service technicians is expected to grow more slowly than the average for all occupations through 2016, according to the U.S. Department of Labor. The reason for this is partly the improving quality and durability of today's electronics products. As manufacturers find ways to make their products better, fewer and less frequent repairs are needed. Two other similar factors figure into this employment decrease as well: lower costs for consumer electronic products, and rapidly evolving technologies. Lower costs make it often more sensible for consumers to replace their malfunctioning equipment than to repair it. Rapidly evolving technologies mean that many consumer electronics products are obsolete by the time they begin to malfunction—and will be replaced by the latest new product. This spurs many consumers to simply move on to the most recent product rather than repair an existing one.

Even with the expected decrease in employment, job opportunities for electronics service technicians should be reasonably good.

This is because there is a fairly high rate of turnover in the profession. Many service technicians leave their jobs to transfer to higher paying positions, such as servicing industrial or office equipment.

FOR MORE INFORMATION

For general information and current news about the electronics industry, contact
AeA (formerly American Electronics Association)
5201 Great America Parkway, Suite 400
Santa Clara, CA 95054-1129
Tel: 800-284-4232
http://www.aeanet.org

For information on educational programs and certification, contact
American Society of Certified Engineering Technicians
PO Box 1536
Brandon, MS 39043-1536
Tel: 601-824-8991
http://www.ascet.org

For specific information on various industry sectors, including consumer electronics, telecommunications, and electronic components, contact or visit the following Web site:
Electronic Industries Alliance
2500 Wilson Boulevard
Arlington, VA 22201-3834
Tel: 703-907-7500
http://www.eia.org

For certification, career, and placement information, contact
Electronics Technicians Association, International
5 Depot Street
Greencastle, IN 46135-8024
Tel: 800-288-3824
Email: eta@eta-i.org
http://www.eta-i.org

For information on student chapters and certification, contact
International Society of Certified Electronics Technicians
3608 Pershing Avenue
Fort Worth, TX 76107-4527
Tel: 800-946-0201
http://www.iscet.org

Hardware Engineers

OVERVIEW

Computer *hardware engineers* design, build, and test computer hardware (such as computer chips and circuit boards) and computer systems. They also work with peripheral devices such as printers, scanners, modems, and monitors, among others. Hardware engineers are employed by a variety of companies, some of which specialize in business, accounting, science, or engineering. Most hardware engineers have a degree in computer science or engineering or equivalent computer background. There are approximately 79,000 computer hardware engineers employed in the United States.

HISTORY

What started as a specialty of electrical engineering has developed into a career field of its own. Today, many individuals interested in a career in one of the computer industry's most promising sectors turn to computer engineering. Computer engineers improve, repair, and implement changes needed to keep up with the demand for faster and stronger computers and complex software programs. Some specialize in the design of the hardware: computer or peripheral parts such as memory chips, motherboards, or microprocessors. Others specialize in creating and organizing information systems for businesses and the government.

More and more businesses rely on computers for information networking, accessing the Internet, and data processing for their daily activities. Also, computers are now affordable, allowing many families to purchase systems. Peripherals, such as printers, scanners, and disk drives, are popular accessories available to complete

School Subjects
Computer science
Mathematics

Personal Skills
Mechanical/manipulative
Technical/scientific

Work Environment
Primarily indoors
Primarily one location

Minimum Education Level
Bachelor's degree

Salary Range
$55,880 to $91,860 to $138,600+

Certification or Licensing
Voluntary

Outlook
Decline

DOT
030

GOE
02.07.01

NOC
2147

O*NET-SOC
17-2061.00

a variety of tasks. Computer engineers are also needed to develop and improve technology needed for consumer products, such as cellular phones, microwave ovens, compact disc players, digital video disc players, high-definition televisions, and video games. Engineers turn to program tools, such as computer-aided design (CAD), to help them create new products. CAD programs are often used with computer-aided manufacturing (CAM) programs to produce three-dimensional drawings that can easily be altered or manipulated, and direct the actual production of hardware components.

THE JOB

Computer hardware engineers work with the physical parts of computers, such as CPUs (computer processing units), motherboards, chipsets, video cards, cooling units, disk drives, storage devices, network cards, and all the components that connect them, down to wires, nuts, and bolts.

Hardware engineers design parts and create prototypes to test, using CAD/CAM technology to make schematic drawings. They assemble the parts using fine hand tools, soldering irons, and microscopes. Parts are reworked and developed through multiple testing procedures. Once a final design is completed, hardware engineers oversee the manufacture and installation of parts.

Computer hardware engineers also work on peripherals, such as keyboards, printers, monitors, mice, track balls, modems, scanners, external storage devices, speaker systems, and digital cameras.

Some hardware engineers are involved in maintenance and repair of computers, networks, and peripherals. They troubleshoot problems, order or make new parts, and install them. Calvin Prior is a network systems administrator for TASC, a nonprofit social service agency headquartered in Chicago, Illinois. He is responsible for the day-to-day operations of a statewide network of more than 300 servers. Prior starts work early; most mornings he's at his desk by 7:30 A.M. His first task of the day is making sure the network files from the previous day backed up successfully. Then he checks for email and voice mail messages and promptly responds to urgent problems.

Daily meetings are held to keep informed on department business. "It's very short and informal," says Prior. "We discuss urgent business or upcoming projects and schedules." The rest of the morning is spent working on various projects, troubleshooting systems, or phone work with TASC's remote offices. After a quick lunch break and if no network breakdowns or glitches occur, Prior usually spends his afternoons researching hardware products or responding to user requests. Since computer technology changes so rapidly, it is important to keep up with the development of new parts and the procedures for incorporating them into older systems as soon as they become available.

The workload changes daily, leaving some days more hectic than others. "It's important to be flexible," says Prior, "and be good at multitasking." If a major problem cannot be solved over the phone, Prior must travel to the source. Solutions are not always simple; some require changing hardware or redesigning the system. Prior often upgrades or reworks systems in the early morning, late at night, or on weekends to minimize the disruption of work. Major network problems require a complete shutdown of the entire system. "The fewer servers on the network, the better," he says.

Engineering professionals like Prior must be familiar with different network systems such as local area networks (LAN), wide area networks (WAN), among others, as well as programming languages suited to their company's needs. Many work as part of a team of specialists who use elements of science, math, and electronics to improve existing technology or implement solutions.

REQUIREMENTS
High School
Calvin Prior credits high school computer and electronics classes and programming courses for giving him a good head start in this career. You should also take math and physics, as well as speech and writing courses so that you will be able to communicate effectively with coworkers and clients.

Postsecondary Training
Hardware engineers need at least a bachelor's degree in computer engineering or electrical engineering. Employment in research laboratories or academic institutions might require a master's or Ph.D. in computer science or engineering. For a list of accredited computer engineering programs, contact the Accreditation Board for Engineering and Technology.

College studies might include such computer science courses as computer architecture, systems design, chip design, microprocessor design, and network architecture, in addition to a heavy concentration of math and science classes.

Certification or Licensing
Not all computer professionals are certified. The deciding factor seems to be if it is required by their employer. Many companies offer tuition reimbursement, or incentives, to those who earn certification. Certification is available in a variety of specialties.

The Institute for Certification of Computing Professionals (ICCP) offers the associate computing professional (ACP) designation for those new to the field and the certified computing professional (CCP) designation for those with at least 48 months of full-time professional-level work in computer-based information systems. Certification is considered by many to be a measure of industry knowledge as well as leverage when negotiating salary.

Other Requirements

Hardware engineers need a broad knowledge of and experience with computer systems and technologies. You need strong problem-solving and analysis skills and good interpersonal skills. Patience, self-motivation, and flexibility are important. Often, a number of projects are worked on simultaneously, so the ability to multitask is important. Because of rapid technological advances in the computer field, continuing education is a necessity.

EMPLOYERS

Approximately 79,000 computer hardware engineers are employed in the United States. Computer hardware engineers are employed in nearly every industry by small and large corporations alike. Approximately 41 percent of hardware engineers are employed in computer and electronic product manufacturing.

Jobs are available nationwide, though salary averages, as reported by a recent Computerworld survey, tend to be higher in New York City and Los Angeles. These cities, however, are notorious for their high cost of living, which, in the end, may offset a higher income.

STARTING OUT

Education and solid work experience will open industry doors. Though a bachelor's degree is a minimum requirement for most corporate giants, some companies, smaller ones especially, will hire based largely on work experience and practical training. Many computer professionals employed in the computer industry for some time do not have traditional electrical engineering or computer science degrees, but rather moved up on the basis of their work record. However, if you aspire to a management position, or want to work as a teacher, then a college degree is a necessity.

Large computer companies aggressively recruit on campus armed with signing bonuses and other incentives. Employment opportunities are posted in newspaper want ads daily, with some papers devoting a separate section to computer-related positions. The Internet offers a wealth of employment information plus several sites for browsing job openings, or to post your resume. Most companies maintain a Web page where they post employment opportunities or solicit resumes.

ADVANCEMENT

Many companies hire new grads to work as junior engineers. Problem-solving skills and the ability to implement solutions is a big part of this entry-level job. With enough work experience, junior engineers can move into positions that focus on a particular area in the computer industry, such as networks or peripherals. Landing a senior-level engineering position, such as systems architect, for example, is possible after considerable work experience and study. Aspiring hardware engineers should hone their computer skills to the highest level through continuing education, certification, or even advanced graduate study. Many high-level engineers hold a master's degree or better.

Some computer professionals working on the technical side of the industry opt to switch over to the marketing side of the business. Advancement opportunities here may include positions in product management or sales.

EARNINGS

Starting salary offers in 2005 for bachelor's degree candidates in computer engineering averaged $56,201, according to a National Association of Colleges and Employers. Master's degree candidates averaged $60,000 and those with Ph.D.'s received $92,500.

The U.S. Department of Labor (USDL) reports that median annual earnings of computer hardware engineers were $91,860 in 2007. Salaries ranged from less than $55,880 to more than $138,600. The USDL reports that hardware engineers earned the following mean salaries by industry: computer and peripheral equipment manufacturing, $99,360; semiconductor and other electronic component manufacturing, $95,820; architectural, engineering, and related services, $94,040; computer systems design and related services, $91,040; and federal executive branch, $90,810.

Job perks, besides the usual benefit package of insurance, vacation, sick time, and profit sharing, may include stock options, continuing education or training, tuition reimbursement, flexible hours, and child care or other on-site services.

WORK ENVIRONMENT

Most hardware engineers work 40- to 50-hour weeks or more depending on the project to which they are assigned. Weekend work is common with some positions. Contrary to popular perceptions, hardware engineers do not spend their workdays cooped up in their offices. Instead, they spend the majority of their time meeting, planning, and working with various staff members from different levels of management and technical expertise. Since it takes numerous workers to take a project from start to finish, team players are in high demand.

OUTLOOK

Employment in hardware engineering will grow more slowly than the average for all occupations through 2016, according to the U.S. Department of Labor. Employment for hardware engineers in computer and electronic product manufacturing is expected to decline during this same time span. Foreign competition and increased productivity at U.S. companies will limit opportunities for hardware engineers. Despite this prediction, opportunities are still expected to be good as the number of new graduates entering the field will match the number of engineers leaving the field. Opportunities will be best for hardware engineers employed in computer systems design and related services.

FOR MORE INFORMATION

For a list of accredited programs in computer engineering, contact
Accreditation Board for Engineering and Technology (ABET)
111 Market Place, Suite 1050
Baltimore, MD 21202 -7116
Tel: 410-347-7700
http://www.abet.org

For information regarding the computer industry, career opportunities as a computer engineer, or the association's membership requirements, contact
Association for Computing Machinery
2 Penn Plaza, Suite 701
New York, NY 10121-0701
Tel: 800-342-6626
Email: acmhelp@acm.org
http://www.acm.org

For information on career opportunities for women in computing, contact

Association for Women in Computing
41 Sutter Street, Suite 1006
San Francisco, CA 94104-5414
Tel: 415-905-4663
Email: info@awc-hq.org
http://www.awc-hq.org

For information on a career in computer engineering and computer scholarships, contact

IEEE Computer Society
2001 L Street, NW, Suite 700
Washington, DC 20036-4910
Tel: 202-371-0101
http://www.computer.org

For information on certification, contact

Institute for Certification of Computing Professionals (ICCP)
2400 East Devon Avenue, Suite 281
Des Plaines, IL 60018-4610
Tel: 800-843-8227
Email: office@iccp.org
http://www.iccp.org

For employment information, links to online career sites for computer professionals, information on membership for college students, and background on the industry, contact

Institute of Electrical and Electronics Engineers (IEEE-USA)
2001 L Street, NW, Suite 700
Washington, DC 20036-4910
Tel: 202-785-0017
Email: ieeeusa@ieee.org
http://www.ieeeusa.org

For comprehensive information about careers in electrical engineering and computer science, visit

Sloan Career Cornerstone Center
http://careercornerstone.org

Industrial Engineers

QUICK FACTS

School Subjects
Computer science
Mathematics

Personal Skills
Leadership/management
Technical/scientific

Work Environment
Primarily indoors
Primarily one location

Minimum Education Level
Bachelor's degree

Salary Range
$46,340 to $71,430 to
$104,490+

Certification or Licensing
Required by certain states

Outlook
About as fast as the average

DOT
012

GOE
02.07.02

NOC
2141

O*NET-SOC
17-2112.00

OVERVIEW

Industrial engineers use their knowledge of various disciplines—including systems engineering, management science, operations research, and fields such as ergonomics—to determine the most efficient and cost-effective methods for industrial production. They are responsible for designing systems that integrate materials, equipment, information, and people in the overall production process. Approximately 201,000 industrial engineers are employed in the United States.

HISTORY

In today's industries, manufacturers increasingly depend on industrial engineers to determine the most efficient production techniques and processes. The roots of industrial engineering, however, can be traced to ancient Greece, where records indicate that manufacturing labor was divided among people having specialized skills.

The most significant milestones in industrial engineering, before the field even had an official name, occurred in the 18th century, when a number of inventions were introduced in the textile industry. The first was the flying shuttle that opened the door to the highly automatic weaving we now take for granted. This shuttle allowed one person, rather than two, to weave fabrics wider than ever before. Other innovative devices, such as the power loom and the spinning jenny that increased weaving speed and improved quality, soon followed. By the late 18th century, the industrial revolution was in full swing. Innovations in manufacturing were made, standardization of interchangeable parts was implemented, and specialization of labor was increasingly put into practice.

Industrial engineering as a science is said to have originated with the work of Frederick Taylor. In 1881, he began to study the way production workers used their time. At the Midvale Steel Company where he was employed, Taylor introduced the concept of time study, whereby workers were timed with a stopwatch and their production was evaluated. He used the studies to design methods and equipment that allowed tasks to be done more efficiently.

In the early 1900s, the field of industrial engineering was known as scientific management. Frank and Lillian Gilbreth were influential with their motion studies of workers performing various tasks. Then, around 1913, automaker Henry Ford implemented a conveyor belt assembly line in his factory, which led to increasingly integrated production lines in more and more companies. Industrial engineers nowadays are called upon to solve even more complex operating problems and to design systems involving large numbers of workers, complicated equipment, and vast amounts of information. They meet this challenge by utilizing advanced computers and software to design complex mathematical models and other simulations.

THE JOB

Industrial engineers are involved with the development and implementation of the systems and procedures that are utilized by many industries and businesses. In general, they figure out the most effective ways to use the three basic elements of any company: people, facilities, and equipment.

Although industrial engineers work in a variety of businesses, the main focus of the discipline is in manufacturing, also called industrial production. Primarily, industrial engineers are concerned with process technology, which includes the design and layout of machinery and the organization of workers who implement the required tasks.

Industrial engineers have many responsibilities. With regard to facilities and equipment, engineers are involved in selecting machinery and other equipment and then in setting them up in the most efficient production layout. They also develop methods to accomplish production tasks, such as the organization of an assembly line. In addition, they devise systems for quality control, distribution, and inventory.

Industrial engineers are responsible for some organizational issues. For instance, they might study an organization chart and other information about a project and then determine the functions and responsibilities of workers. They devise and implement job evaluation procedures as well as articulate labor utilization standards for workers. Engineers often meet with managers to discuss cost analysis, financial planning, job evaluation, and salary administration. Not only do they recommend methods for improving employee efficiency, but they may also devise wage and incentive programs.

Industrial engineers evaluate ergonomic issues, the relationship between human capabilities and the physical environment in which they work. For example, they might evaluate whether machines are causing physical harm or discomfort to workers or whether the machines could be designed differently to enable workers to be more productive.

REQUIREMENTS

High School

To prepare for a college engineering program, concentrate on mathematics (algebra, trigonometry, geometry, calculus), physical sciences (physics, chemistry), social sciences (economics, sociology), and English. Engineers often have to convey ideas graphically and may need to visualize processes in three-dimension, so courses in graphics, drafting, or design are also helpful. In addition, round out your education with computer science, history, and foreign language classes. If honors-level courses are available to you, be sure to take them.

Postsecondary Training

A bachelor's degree from an accredited institution is usually the minimum requirement for all professional positions. The Accreditation Board for Engineering and Technology (ABET) accredits schools offering engineering programs, including industrial engineering. A listing of accredited colleges and universities is available on the ABET's Web site (http://www.abet.org), and a visit there should be one of your first stops when you are deciding on a school to attend. Colleges and universities offer either four- or five-year engineering programs. Because of the intensity of the curricula, many students take heavy course loads and attend summer sessions in order to finish in four years.

During your junior and senior years of college, you should consider your specific career goals, such as in which industry to work. Third- and fourth-year courses focus on such subjects as facility planning and design, work measurement standards, process design, engineering economics, manufacturing and automation, and incentive plans.

Many industrial engineers go on to earn a graduate degree. These programs tend to involve more research and independent study. Graduate degrees are usually required for teaching positions.

Certification or Licensing

Licensure as a professional engineer is recommended since an increasing number of employers require it. Even those employers who do not require licensing will view it favorably when considering new hires or when reviewing workers for promotion. Licensing requirements vary from state to state. In general, however, they involve having graduated from an accredited school, having four years of work experience, and having passed the eight-hour Fundamentals of Engineering exam and the eight-hour Principles and Practice of Engineering exam. These exams are offered by the National Council of Examiners for Engineering and Surveying (http://www.ncees.org). Depending on your state, you can take the Fundamentals exam shortly before your graduation from college or after you have received your bachelor's degree. At that point you will be an engineer-in-training. Once you have fulfilled all the licensure requirements, you receive the designation professional engineer.

Other Requirements

Industrial engineers enjoy problem solving and analyzing things as well as being a team member. The ability to communicate is vital since engineers interact with all levels of management and workers. Being organized and detail minded is important because industrial engineers often handle large projects and must bring them in on time and on budget. Since process design is the cornerstone of the field, an engineer should be creative and inventive.

EXPLORING

Try joining a science or engineering club, such as the Junior Engineering Technical Society (JETS). JETS offers academic competitions in subjects such as computer fundamentals, mathematics, physics, and English. It also conducts design contests in which students learn and apply science and engineering principles. JETS also offers the *Pre-Engineering Times*, a publication that will be useful if you are interested in engineering. It contains information on engineering specialties, competitions, schools, scholarships, and other resources. Visit http://www.jets.org/publications/petimes.cfm to read the publication.

You also might read some engineering books for background on the field or magazines such as *Industrial Engineer,* a magazine published by the Institute of Industrial Engineers (IIE). Selected articles from *Industrial Engineer* can be viewed on the IIE's Web site (http://www.iienet.org).

EMPLOYERS

Approximately 201,000 industrial engineers are employed in the United States. Although a majority of industrial engineers are employed in the manufacturing industry, related jobs are found in almost all businesses, including aviation, aerospace, transportation, communications, electric, gas and sanitary services, government, finance, insurance, real estate, wholesale and retail trade, construction, mining, agriculture, forestry, and fishing. Also, many work as independent consultants.

STARTING OUT

The main qualification for an entry-level job is a bachelor's degree in industrial engineering. Accredited college programs generally have job openings listed in their career services offices. Entry-level industrial engineers find jobs in various departments, such as computer operations, warehousing, and quality control. As engineers gain on-the-job experience and familiarity with departments, they may decide on a specialty. Some may want to continue to work as process designers or methods engineers, while others may move on to administrative positions.

Some further examples of specialties include work measurement standards, shipping and receiving, cost control, engineering economics, materials handling, management information systems, mathematical models, and operations. Many who choose industrial engineering as a career find its appeal in the diversity of sectors that are available to explore.

ADVANCEMENT

After having worked at least three years in the same job, an industrial engineer may have the basic credentials needed for advancement to a higher position. In general, positions in operations and administration are considered high-level jobs, although this varies from company to company. Engineers who work in these areas tend to earn larger salaries than those who work in warehousing or cost control, for example. If one is interested in moving to a different company, it is considered easier to do so within the same industry.

Industrial engineering jobs are often considered stepping-stones to management positions, even in other fields. Engineers with many years' experience frequently are promoted to higher level jobs with greater responsibilities. Because of the field's broad exposure, industrial engineering employees are generally considered better prepared for executive roles than are other types of engineers.

EARNINGS

According to a survey by the National Association of Colleges and Employers, the average starting salary for industrial engineers with a bachelor's degree was $55,067 in 2007, with a master's degree, $64,759 a year; and with a Ph.D., $77,364.

According to the U.S. Department of Labor (USDL), the median annual wage for industrial engineers in 2007 was $71,430. The lowest paid 10 percent of all industrial engineers earned less than $46,340 annually. However, as with most occupations, salaries rise as more experience is gained. Very experienced engineers can earn more than $104,490. The USDL reports the following mean earnings for industrial engineers by industry sector: semiconductor and other electronic component manufacturing, $79,850; navigational, measuring, electromedical, and control instruments manufacturing, $77,510; and aerospace product and parts manufacturing, $75,090.

Benefits for full-time industrial engineers include vacation and sick time, health and dental insurance, and pension or 401(k) plans.

WORK ENVIRONMENT

Industrial engineers usually work in offices at desks and computers, designing and evaluating plans, statistics, and other documents. Overall, industrial engineering is ranked above other engineering disciplines for factors such as employment outlook, salary, and physical environment. However, industrial engineering jobs are considered stressful because they often entail tight deadlines and demanding quotas, and jobs are moderately competitive. Most engineers work an average of 40 hours per week.

Industrial engineers generally collaborate with other employees, conferring on designs and procedures, as well as with business managers and consultants. Although they spend most of their time in their offices, they frequently must evaluate conditions at factories and plants, where noise levels are often high.

OUTLOOK

The U.S. Department of Labor anticipates that employment for industrial engineers will grow faster than the average for all occupations through 2016. Employment for industrial engineers in computer and electronic product manufacturing is expected to grow about as fast as the average during this same time span. The demand for industrial engineers will continue as manufacturing and other companies strive to make their production processes more effective and competitive. Engineers who transfer or retire will create the highest percentage of openings in this field.

FOR MORE INFORMATION

For a list of ABET-accredited engineering schools, contact
Accreditation Board for Engineering and Technology (ABET)
111 Market Place, Suite 1050
Baltimore, MD 21202-7116
Tel: 410-347-7700
http://www.abet.org

For comprehensive information about careers in industrial engineering, contact
Institute of Industrial Engineers
3577 Parkway Lane, Suite 200
Norcross, GA 30092-2833
Tel: 800-494-0460
http://www.iienet.org

Visit the JETS Web site for membership information and to read the online brochure Industrial Engineering.
Junior Engineering Technical Society (JETS)
1420 King Street, Suite 405
Alexandria, VA 22314-2750
Tel: 703-548-5387
Email: info@jets.org
http://www.jets.org

━━━━━ INTERVIEW ━━━━━

Emma Fulton works as an industrial engineer for the Intel Corporation in Chandler, Arizona. She discussed her career with the editors of Careers in Focus: Electronics.

Q. What is your job title? Where do you work?
A. Arizona Fab Sort Manufacturing (AZFSM) Factory Industrial Engineer; AZFSM is comprised of Intel's three semiconductor fabrication facilities in Chandler—Fab 12, Fab 22, and Fab 32. I work on projects in all three factories on a regular basis.

Q. How long have you worked in the field?
A. Three years full time. I also did a year of co-ops during college: five months at Intel, five months at General Mills making cereal, and three months at General Electric making refrigerators.

Q. What made you want to enter this career?

A. I was looking at Intel as a possible employer due to their company ethics, locations, flexibility, diversity initiatives, and stability of employment. I wanted to be proud to wear a company shirt. I found that Intel needed to locate its facilities in big cities to draw sufficient talent, and I love big cities. Growing up just outside New York City, I was not interested in working in rural areas.

Semiconductor plants are probably *the* most complex systems in the world. It takes weeks to produce a completed wafer, whereas cereal is done within hours. In other words, I would forever find challenges at work.

Oh, and did I mention I froze during college at Rochester Institute of Technology in Rochester, New York? I wanted to be warm, which Chandler certainly is.

Q. What are some of the pros and cons of your job?

A. We are a 24/7 facility, which is both a pro and a con. Our factories require engineering support around the clock, necessitating a variety of schedules. Many engineers work a compressed shift schedule, alternating three- and four-day weeks with 12-hour days; there are two day shifts and two night shifts. I have friends who work Wednesday through Saturday and other friends who work Sunday through Tuesday. Parents who both work at Intel find the scheduling can be a tall hurdle, especially getting on the same shift or complementary shifts. However, the scheduling could mean three- or four-day weekends *every* weekend. So you see why the scheduling can be good or bad.

Intel has a great structure to ensure job training is available. I can study material posted on the Internet as well as take classes in a conventional classroom with on-site instructors. I can take classes relating to my current job or the job I would like to have in the future. At Intel, job rotations are common, as every seven years an employee earns a two-month sabbatical, which typically means that someone must fill in. Therefore, the organization must adapt seamlessly to frequent changes.

I work daily with many industrial engineers. I learn from them, and they learn from me. I have classmates from college working for other companies who are the only engineer in their facility. I enjoy having many colleagues, but there is a risk of overlapping work.

Q. What are the most important personal and professional qualities for people in your career?

A. • Organization skills
  • Communications skills (written and oral, in particular the ability to speak confidently and smoothly to groups up to 75 people)

- Teamwork skills (ability to work well with others)
- Flexibility/adaptability
- Strong work ethic

Q. What advice would you give to high school and college students who are interested in the field?

A. Industrial engineering (IE) is a very diverse and broad field. It's also poorly understood by those outside the profession, so do your research. (Suggested research: Read *Cheaper by the Dozen* about one of the pioneers in the field, Frank Gilbreth, and *The Goal: A Process of Ongoing Improvement* by Eliyahu M. Goldratt and Jeff Cox; and visit http://www.iienet.org.) Think about what you want in life. If you don't like to fly, don't become an aeronautical engineer. Similarly, if you enjoy optimizing systems and making them run more smoothly, then being an industrial engineer might suit you.

It's encouraging knowing that an industrial engineer has job choices all over the world, in many industries, and applying different sets of IE skills. Consider your options and how well the attributes of the profession correspond with your life interests.

Inspectors

OVERVIEW

Electronics inspectors, sometimes known as *testers,* inspect electronic and electromechanical assemblies, subassemblies, components, and parts to ensure that they meet prescribed specifications.

HISTORY

Quality control inspection is an outgrowth of the industrial revolution. As it began in England in the 18th century, each person involved in the manufacturing process was responsible for a particular part of the process. The worker's responsibility was further specialized by the introduction of the concept of interchangeable parts in the late 18th and early 19th centuries. In a manufacturing process using this concept (such as in the automotive industry, for example), a worker could focus on making just one component, while other workers concentrated on creating other components. Such specialization led to increased production efficiency, especially as manufacturing processes became mechanized during the early part of the 20th century. It also meant, however, that no one worker was responsible for the overall quality of the product. This led to the need for another kind of specialized production worker whose primary responsibility was not one aspect of the product but rather its overall quality.

This responsibility initially belonged to the mechanical engineers and technicians who developed the manufacturing systems, equipment, and procedures. After World War II, however, a new field emerged that was dedicated solely to quality control. Along with specially trained persons to test and inspect products coming off assembly lines, new instruments, equipment, and techniques were developed to measure and monitor specified standards.

QUICK FACTS

School Subjects
Mathematics
Technical/shop

Personal Skills
Communication/ideas
Technical/scientific

Work Environment
Indoors and outdoors
Primarily one location

Minimum Education Level
Some postsecondary training

Salary Range
$18,630 to $35,000 to $52,230+

Certification or Licensing
Voluntary

Outlook
Decline

DOT
726

GOE
08.02.03

NOC
2244, 9482

O*NET-SOC
51-9061.00

At first, inspectors were primarily responsible for random checks of products to ensure they met all specifications. This usually entailed testing and inspecting either finished products or products at various stages of production.

During the 1980s, a renewed emphasis on quality spread across the United States. Faced with increased global competition, especially from Japanese auto manufacturers, many U.S. automotive companies sought to improve quality and productivity. Quality improvement concepts such as Total Quality Management, Six Sigma, continuous improvement, quality circles, and zero defects gained popularity and changed the way in which companies viewed quality and quality control practices. A new philosophy emerged, emphasizing quality as the concern of all individuals involved in producing goods and directing that quality be monitored at all stages of manufacturing, not just at the end of production or at random stages of manufacturing.

THE JOB

Electronics inspectors ensure that electronic and electromechanical assemblies, subassemblies, components (such as diodes, switches, and resistors), and parts meet prescribed specifications. They consult schematics and blueprints and use precision measuring instruments to inspect electrical and electronics systems such as automobile ignition and fuel injection systems, avionics systems in commercial airliners, and semiconductors and other electronic components used in the assembly of computers, iPods, and other technologies. Inspectors have a wide range of responsibilities. For example, they ensure that the materials used in the manufacturing process are free of defects, that electronic components are wired and soldered properly, and that manufacturing specifications and contract requirements are met. They also conduct life tests (sometimes called burn-ins) on assemblies, subassemblies, and components. This test uses electrical stimulation to accelerate the lifetime of a component or product to see if it works effectively during its anticipated shelf life. Products that fail this test are removed from production before distribution. If a large number of a particular product fail a burn-in or other test, inspectors may revise a manufacturing or installation process to avoid future defects or deviations in specifications. They often meet with other members of the manufacturing or production team to identify weakness in the design or manufacturing of a product.

Electronics inspectors are often employed by electronics, aviation, aerospace, and other manufacturers, although some may find work with companies that contract out their various inspection services.

A manufacturing inspector verifies defects and repairs circuit lines in semiconductor chips. *(Stephen D. Cannerelli/Syracuse Newspapers, The Image Works)*

REQUIREMENTS

High School

To prepare for the field, high school students should focus on general classes in speech; English, especially writing; business; computer science; general mathematics; physics; and shop or vocational training.

Postsecondary Training

Electronics inspectors typically receive on-the-job training, but may also complete two- or four-year degree programs in quality assurance or quality control management. For federal positions, a civil service examination is generally required. Education and experience in the specific field is usually necessary.

Certification or Licensing

Although there are no licensing or certification requirements designed specifically for electronics inspectors, many inspectors pursue the voluntary quality inspector certification from the American Society for Quality. Requirements include having a certain amount of work or educational experience and passing a written examination. Many employers value this certification and take it into consideration when making new hires or giving promotions.

Other Requirements

Electronics inspectors must be precision minded, have an eye for detail, and be able to accept responsibility. They also must be able to communicate well with others to reach a clear analysis of a situation and be able to report this information to a superior or coworker. Inspectors must be able to write effective reports that convey vast amounts of information and investigative work.

EXPLORING

If you are interested in work as an electronics inspector, you may learn more by talking with people who are employed as inspectors and with your high school counselor. Employment at an electronics manufacturing plant during summer vacations could be valuable preparation, giving you the opportunity to meet and perhaps talk with inspectors about their careers.

EMPLOYERS

Electronics inspectors are employed in the computer and electronic product, automotive, aviation, aerospace, and other manufacturing industries. Other inspectors are employed by local, state, and federal governments.

STARTING OUT

College students may learn of openings for inspectors through their schools' career services office. Recruiters often visit these schools and interview graduating students for technical positions. Students may also learn about openings through help wanted ads or by using the services of state and private employment services. They also may apply directly to electronics manufacturers.

ADVANCEMENT

As electronics inspectors gain experience or additional education, they are given more responsible assignments. Promotion usually depends on additional training as well as job performance. Inspectors who obtain additional training have greater chances for advancement opportunities. Inspectors who work for electronics companies with large staffs of inspection personnel can become managers or advance to operations management positions.

EARNINGS

According to the U.S. Department of Labor (USDL), salaries for inspectors, testers, sorters, samplers, and weighers ranged from less than $18,630 to $52,230 or more annually in 2007. The USDL reports the following mean salaries for inspectors, testers, sorters, samplers, and weighers by industry sector: aerospace products and parts manufacturing, $45,020; motor vehicle parts manufacturing, $38,300; and semiconductor and other electronic component manufacturing, $31,030.

Electronics inspectors receive benefits including paid vacation and sick days, health and dental insurance, pensions, and life insurance.

WORK ENVIRONMENT

Some electronics inspectors work in manufacturing plants, where conditions may be hot, dirty, and noisy. Others work in laboratories or workshops where they test and inspect raw materials, microchips, and other substances. Because many manufacturing plants operate 24 hours a day, some inspectors may need to work second or third shifts.

OUTLOOK

The U.S. Department of Labor predicts that the employment of inspectors, testers, sorters, samplers, and weighers will decline through 2016 because of increased automation of quality control and testing procedures. Most job opportunities will arise as a result of people retiring, transferring to other positions, and leaving the labor force for a variety of other reasons.

FOR MORE INFORMATION

For information on certification, contact
American Society for Quality
PO Box 3005
Milwaukee, WI 53201-3005
Tel: 800-248-1946
Email: help@asq.org
http://www.asq.org

Mechanical Engineers

OVERVIEW

Mechanical engineers plan and design tools, engines, machines, and other mechanical systems that produce, transmit, or use power. They may work in design, instrumentation, testing, robotics, transportation, or bioengineering, among other areas. The broadest of all engineering disciplines, mechanical engineering extends across many interdependent specialties. Mechanical engineers may work in production operations, maintenance, or technical sales, and many are administrators or managers. There are approximately 227,000 mechanical engineers employed in the United States.

HISTORY

The modern field of mechanical engineering took root during the Renaissance. In this period, engineers focused their energies on developing more efficient ways to perform such ordinary tasks as grinding grain and pumping water. Water wheels and windmills were common energy producers at that time. Leonardo da Vinci, who attempted to design such complex machines as a submarine and a helicopter, best personified the burgeoning mechanical inventiveness of the period. One of the Renaissance's most significant inventions was the mechanical clock, powered first by falling weights and later by compressed springs.

Despite these developments, it was not until the industrial revolution that mechanical engineering took on its modern form. The steam engine, an efficient power producer, was introduced in 1712 by Thomas Newcomen to pump water from English mines. More than a half century later, James Watt modified Newcomen's engine to power industrial machines. In 1876, a German, Nicolaus Otto, developed the internal combustion engine, which became one of the century's most important inventions. In 1847, a group of British engineers who specialized in steam engines and machine tools, organized the Institution of Mechanical Engineers. The American Society of Mechanical Engineers (now known as ASME International) was founded in 1880.

Mechanical engineering rapidly expanded in the 20th century. Mass production systems allowed large quantities of standardized goods to be made at a low cost, and mechanical engineers played a pivotal role in the design of these systems. In the second half of the 20th century, computers revolutionized production. Mechanical engineers now design mechanical systems on computers, and they are used to test, monitor, and analyze mechanical systems and factory production. Mechanical engineers are key players in countless industries, including the computer and electronics manufacturing industries.

THE JOB

The work of a mechanical engineer begins with research and development. An electronics company, for example, may need to develop a new design for a clean room that features improved heating and air-conditioning, plumbing, and fire protection systems or create new process systems (chillers, scrubbers, exhaust, etc.) in a semiconductor manufacturing plant. A research engineer explores the project's theoretical, mechanical, and material problems. The engineer may perform experiments to gather necessary data and acquire new knowledge. Often, an experimental device or system is developed.

The *design engineer* takes information gained from research and development and uses it to plan a product or system. The engineer would be responsible for specifying every detail of the machine or mechanical system. Since the introduction of sophisticated software programs, mechanical engineers have increasingly used computers in the design process.

After the product or system has been designed and a prototype developed, the product is analyzed by *testing engineers*. A manufacturing system, for example, would need to be tested for temperature, vibration, dust, and performance, as well as for any government safety regulations. If dust is penetrating a bearing, the testing engineer would refer the problem to the design engineer, who would then make an adjustment to the design of the transmission. Design and testing engineers continue to work together until the product meets the necessary criteria.

Once the final design is set, it is the job of the *manufacturing engineer* to come up with the most time- and cost-efficient way of making the product or system without sacrificing quality. The amount of factory floor space, the type of manufacturing equipment and machinery, and the cost of labor and materials are some of the factors that must be considered. Engineers select the necessary equipment and machines and oversee their arrangement and safe operation. Other engineering specialists, such as chemical, electrical, and industrial engineers, may provide assistance.

Some types of mechanical systems (from factory machinery to nuclear power plants) are so sophisticated that mechanical engineers are needed for operation and ongoing maintenance. With the help of computers, *maintenance and operations engineers* use their specialized knowledge to monitor complex production systems and make necessary adjustments.

Mechanical engineers also work in marketing, sales, and administration. Because of their training in mechanical engineering, *sales engineers* can give customers a detailed explanation of how a machine or system works. They may also be able to alter its design to meet a customer's needs.

In a small company, a mechanical engineer may need to perform many, if not most, of the above responsibilities. Some tasks might be assigned to *consulting engineers,* who are either self-employed or work for a consulting firm. At large government organizations, a mechanical engineer may just focus on one of the above responsibilities.

REQUIREMENTS

High School

If you are interested in mechanical engineering as a career, you need to take courses in geometry, trigonometry, and calculus. Physics and chemistry courses are also recommended, as is mechanical drawing or computer-aided design, if they are offered at your high school. Communications skills are important for mechanical engineers because they interact with a variety of coworkers and vendors and are often required to prepare and/or present reports. English and speech classes are also helpful. Finally, because computers are such an important part of engineering, computer science courses are good choices.

Postsecondary Training

A bachelor's degree in mechanical engineering is usually the minimum educational requirement for entering this field. A master's degree, or even a Ph.D., may be necessary to obtain some positions, such as those in research, teaching, and administration.

In the United States, more than 280 colleges and universities have mechanical engineering programs that have been approved by the Accreditation Board for Engineering and Technology. Although admissions requirements vary slightly from school to school, most require a solid background in mathematics and science.

In a four-year undergraduate program, students typically begin by studying mathematics and science subjects, such as calculus, differential equations, physics, and chemistry. Course work in liberal arts and elementary mechanical engineering is also taken. By the third year, students begin to study the technical core subjects of mechanical engineering—mechanics, thermodynamics, fluid mechanics, design manufacturing, and heat transfer—as well as such specialized topics as power generation and transmission, computer-aided design systems, and the properties of materials.

At some schools, a five- or six-year program combines classroom study with practical experience working for an engineering firm or a government agency such as NASA. Although these cooperative, or work study, programs take longer, they offer significant advantages. Not only does the salary help pay for educational expenses, but the student has the opportunity to apply theoretical knowledge to actual work problems in mechanical engineering. In some cases, the company or government agency may offer full-time employment to its co-op workers after graduation.

A graduate degree is a prerequisite for becoming a university professor or researcher. It may also lead to a higher-level job within an engineering department or firm. Some companies encourage their employees to pursue graduate education by offering tuition-reimbursement programs. Because technology is rapidly developing, mechanical engineers need to continue their education, formally or informally, throughout their careers. Conferences, seminars, and professional journals serve to educate engineers about developments in the field.

Certification or Licensing

Engineers whose work may affect the life, health, or safety of the public must be registered according to regulations in all 50 states and the District of Columbia. Applicants for registration must have received a degree from an accredited engineering program and have four years of experience. They must also pass a written examination.

Many mechanical engineers also become certified. Certification is a status granted by a technical or professional organization for the purpose of recognizing and documenting an individual's abilities in a specific engineering field. For example, the Society of Manufacturing Engineers offers the following designations to mechanical engineers who work in manufacturing and who meet education and experience requirements: certified manufacturing engineer and certified engineer manager.

Other Requirements

Personal qualities essential for mechanical engineers include the ability to think analytically, to solve problems, and to work with abstract ideas. Attention to detail is also important, as are good oral and written communications skills and the ability to work well in groups. Computer literacy is essential.

EXPLORING

One of the best ways to learn about the field is to talk with a mechanical engineer. Public libraries usually have books on mechanical engineering that might be enlightening. You might tackle a design or building project to test your aptitude for the field. Finally, some high schools offer engineering clubs or organizations. Membership in JETS, the Junior Engineering Technical Society (http://www.jets.org), is suggested for prospective mechanical engineers.

EMPLOYERS

Approximately 227,000 mechanical engineers are employed in the United States, with about 9 percent of this number employed in computer and electronic product manufacturing. Mechanical engineers also work in a variety of other settings, including private engineering and aerospace companies, government entities such as NASA and the U.S. Department of Defense, and manufacturers of industrial and office machinery, farm equipment, automobiles, petroleum, pharmaceuticals, fabricated metal products, pulp and paper, utilities, soap and cosmetics, and heating, ventilating, and air-conditioning systems. Others are self-employed or work for colleges and universities.

STARTING OUT

Many mechanical engineers find their first job through their college or university career services office. Many companies send recruiters to college campuses to interview and sign up engineering graduates. Other students might find a position in the company where they had a summer or part-time job. Newspapers and professional journals often list job openings for engineers.

Books to Read

Bird, John, and Carl T. F. Ross. *Mechanical Engineering Principles.* New York: Newnes, 2002.

Karl-Heinrich Grote, and Erik K. Antonsson, eds. *Springer Handbook of Mechanical Engineering.* New York: Springer Publishing Company, 2008.

Kreith, Frank, and D. Yogi Goswami, eds. *The CRC Handbook of Mechanical Engineering.* 2d ed. Boca Raton, Fla.: CRC Press, 2004.

Wickert, Jonathan. *An Introduction to Mechanical Engineering.* 2d ed. Florence, Ky.: Cengage-Engineering, 2005.

ADVANCEMENT

As engineers gain experience, they can advance to jobs with a wider scope of responsibility and higher pay. Some of these higher-level jobs include technical service and development officers, team leaders, research directors, and managers. Some mechanical engineers use their technical knowledge in sales and marketing positions, while others form their own engineering business or consulting firm.

Many engineers advance by furthering their education. A master's degree in business administration, in addition to an engineering degree, is sometimes helpful in obtaining an administrative position. A master's or doctoral degree in an engineering specialty may also lead to executive work. In addition, those with graduate degrees often have the option of research or teaching positions.

EARNINGS

The National Association of Colleges and Employers reports the following 2007 starting salaries for mechanical engineers by educational achievement: bachelor's degree, $54,128; master's degree, $62,798; and Ph.D., $72,763.

The U.S. Department of Labor reports the following mean earnings for mechanical engineers by industry specialty: scientific research and development services, $86,480; navigational, measuring, electromedical, and control instruments manufacturing, $79,790; and architectural, engineering, and related services, $78,620. Mechanical engineers employed in all industries earned salaries that ranged from less than $46,560 to $108,740 or more in 2007.

Like most professionals, mechanical engineers who work for a company or for a government agency usually receive a generous benefits package, including vacation days, sick leave, health and life insurance, and a savings and pension program. Self-employed mechanical engineers must provide their own benefits.

WORK ENVIRONMENT

The working conditions of mechanical engineers vary. Most mechanical engineers work indoors in offices, research laboratories, or production departments of factories and shops. Depending on the job, however, a significant amount of work time may be spent on a noisy factory floor, at a construction site, or at another field operation. Mechanical engineers have traditionally designed systems on drafting boards, but since the introduction of sophisticated software programs, design is increasingly done on computers.

Engineering is for the most part a cooperative effort. While the specific duties of an engineer may require independent work, each project is typically the job of an engineering team. Such a team might include other engineers, engineering technicians, and engineering technologists.

Mechanical engineers generally have a 40-hour workweek; however, their working hours are often dictated by project deadlines. They may work long hours to meet a deadline, or show up on a second or third shift to check production at a factory or a construction project.

Mechanical engineering can be a very satisfying occupation. Engineers often get the pleasure of seeing their designs or modifications put into actual, tangible form, such as a satellite system or a new type of computer server. Conversely, it can be frustrating when a project is stalled, full of errors, or even abandoned completely.

OUTLOOK

The employment of mechanical engineers is expected to grow more slowly than the average for all occupations through 2016, according to the U.S. Department of Labor (USDL). The employment of mechanical engineers in computer and electronic product manufacturing is expected to decline during this same time span. Although overall employment in manufacturing is expected to decline, engineers will be needed to meet the demand for more efficient industrial machinery and machine tools. The USDL predicts good opportunities for mechanical engineers who are involved with new technologies such as biotechnology, nanotechnology, and materials science. Increases in defense spending as a result of the wars in Iraq and

Afghanistan may create improved employment opportunities for engineers within the federal government.

FOR MORE INFORMATION

For a list of engineering programs at colleges and universities, contact
Accreditation Board for Engineering and Technology
111 Market Place, Suite 1050
Baltimore, MD 21202-4012
Tel: 410-347-7700
http://www.abet.org

For information on mechanical engineering and mechanical engineering technology, contact
ASME International
Three Park Avenue
New York, NY 10016-5990
Tel: 800-843-2763
Email: infocentral@asme.org
http://www.asme.org

For career and scholarship information, contact
General Aviation Manufacturers Association
1400 K Street, NW, Suite 801
Washington, DC 20005-2402
Tel: 202-393-1500
http://www.gama.aero/home.php

For information about careers and high school engineering competitions, contact
Junior Engineering Technical Society
1420 King Street, Suite 405
Alexandria, VA 22314-2794
Tel: 703-548-5387
Email: info@jets.org
http://www.jets.org

For information on certification, contact
Society of Manufacturing Engineers
One SME Drive
Dearborn, MI 48121-2408
Tel: 800-733-4763
http://www.sme.org

Microelectronics Technicians

QUICK FACTS

School Subjects
English
Mathematics
Physics

Personal Skills
Mechanical/manipulative
Technical/scientific

Work Environment
Primarily indoors
Primarily one location

Minimum Education Level
Associate's degree

Salary Range
$31,310 to $52,140 to
$85,000

Certification or Licensing
Voluntary

Outlook
More slowly than the average

DOT
590

GOE
08.02.02

NOC
9483

O*NET-SOC
17-3023.00

OVERVIEW

Microelectronics technicians work in research laboratories assisting the engineering staff to develop and construct prototype and custom-designed microchips. Microchips, often called simply chips, are tiny but extremely complex electronic devices that control the operations of many kinds of communications equipment, consumer products, industrial controls, aerospace guidance systems, and medical electronics. The process of manufacturing chips is also called fabrication. Microelectronics technicians are often classified under the career category, electrical and electronics engineering technician. About 170,000 people work as electrical and electronics engineering technicians.

HISTORY

The science of electronics is only about 100 years old. Yet electronics has had an enormous impact on the way people live. Without electronics, things like television, telephones, computers, X-ray machines, and radar would not be possible. Today, nearly every area of industry, manufacturing, entertainment, health care, and communications uses electronics to improve the quality of people's lives. This article you are reading, for example, was created by people using electronic equipment, from the writing of each article to the design, layout, and production of the book itself.

The earliest electronic systems depended on electron vacuum tubes to conduct current. But these devices were too bulky and too slow for many of their desired tasks. In the early 1950s, the introduction of microelectronics—that is, the design and production of integrated circuits and products using integrated circuits—allowed engineers and scientists to design faster and faster and smaller and smaller electronic devices. Initially developed for military equipment and space technology, integrated circuits have made possible such everyday products as personal computers, microwave ovens, and digital video disc players and are found in nearly every electronic product that people use today.

Integrated circuits are miniaturized electronic systems. Integrated circuits include many interconnected electronic components such as transistors, capacitors, and resistors, produced on or in a single thin slice of a semiconductor material. Semiconductors are so named because they are substances with electrical properties somewhere between those of conductors and insulators. The semiconductor used most frequently in microchips is silicon, so microchips are also sometimes called silicon chips. Often smaller than a fingernail, chips may contain multiple layers of complex circuitry stacked on top of each other. The word integrated refers to the way the circuitry is blended into the chip during the fabrication process.

The reliance on electronic technology has created a need for skilled personnel to design, construct, test, and repair electronic components and products. The growing uses of microelectronics has created a corresponding demand for technicians specially trained to assist in the design and development of new applications of electronic technology.

THE JOB

Microelectronics technicians typically assist in the development of prototypes, or new kinds, of electronic components and products. They work closely with electronics engineers, who design the components, build and test them, and prepare the component or product for large-scale manufacture. Such components usually require the integrated operation of many different types of chips.

Microelectronics technicians generally work from a schematic received from the design engineer. The schematic contains a list of the parts that will be needed to construct the component and the layout that the technician will follow. The technician gathers the parts and prepares the materials to be used. Following the schematic, the technician constructs the component and then uses a variety of sophisticated, highly sensitive equipment to test the component's performance. One such test measures the component's burn-in time.

During this test the component is kept in continuous operation for a long period of time, and the component and its various features are subjected to a variety of tests to be certain the component will stand up to extended use.

If the component fails to function according to its required specifications, the microelectronics technician must be able to troubleshoot the design, locating where the component has failed, and replace one part for a new or different part. Test results are reported to the engineering staff, and the technician may be required to help evaluate the results and prepare reports based on these evaluations. In many situations, the microelectronics technician will work closely with the engineer to solve any problems arising in the component's operation and design.

After the testing period, the microelectronics technician is often responsible for assisting in the technical writing of the component's specifications. These specifications are used for integrating the component into new or redesigned products or for developing the process for the component's large-scale manufacture. The microelectronics technician helps to develop the production system for the component and will also write reports on the component's functions, uses, and performance.

"You really need to have good communications skills," says Kyle Turner, a microelectronics technician at White Oak Semiconductor in Virginia. "Not only do you have to let others know what you mean and explain yourself, you often have to train new employees in the specifics of our product."

Microelectronics technicians perform many of the same functions of electronics technicians, but generally work only in the development laboratory. More experienced technicians may assume greater responsibilities. They work closely with the engineering staff to develop layout and assembly procedures and to use their own knowledge of microelectronics to suggest changes in circuitry or installation. Often they are depended upon to simplify the assembly or maintenance requirements. After making any changes, they test the performance of the component, analyze the results, and suggest and perform further modifications to the component's design. Technicians may fabricate new parts using various machine tools, supervise the installation of the new component, or become involved in training and supervising other technical personnel.

Some microelectronics technicians specialize in the fabrication and testing of semiconductors and integrated circuits. These technicians are usually called *semiconductor development technicians*. They are involved in the development of prototype chips, following the direction of engineering staff, and perform the various steps required for making and testing new integrated circuits.

REQUIREMENTS

The advanced technology involved in microelectronics means that post-high school education or training is a requirement for entering the field. You should consider enrolling in a two-year training program at a community college or vocational training facility and expect to earn a certificate or an associate's degree. Like most microelectronics technicians, Kyle Turner completed a two-year degree in electronics as well as an extensive on-the-job training program.

High School

High school students interested in microelectronics can begin their preparation by taking courses such as algebra and geometry. If you have taken science courses, especially chemistry and physics, you will have a better chance to enter an apprenticeship program and you will be more prepared for postsecondary educational programs.

"Math skills are really important," says Turner. "You have to be able to take accurate measurements and make good calculations."

Knowledge of proper grammar and spelling is necessary for writing reports, and you should also develop your reading comprehension. Taking industrial classes, such as metalworking, wood shop, auto shop, and machine shop, and similar courses in plastics, electronics, and construction techniques will be helpful. Another area of study is computer science, and you would do well to seek experience in computer technology.

Postsecondary Training

Few employers will hire people for microelectronics technician positions who do not have advanced training. Although some low-skilled workers may advance into technician jobs, employers generally prefer to hire people with higher education. Technician and associate's degree programs are available at many community colleges and at public and private vocational training centers and schools. Many technical schools are located where the microelectronics industry is particularly active. These schools often have programs tailored specifically for the needs of companies in their area. Community colleges offer a greater degree of flexibility in that they are able to keep up with the rapid advances and changes in technology and can redesign their courses and programs to meet the new requirements. You can expect to study in such areas as mathematics, including algebra, geometry, and calculus; physics; and electronics engineering technology. Many schools will require you to take courses in English composition, as well as fulfill other course requirements in the humanities and social sciences.

Other methods of entry are three- and four-year apprenticeship programs. These programs generally involve on-the-job training by the employer. You can locate apprenticeship opportunities through your high school guidance office, in listings in local newspapers, or by contacting local manufacturers.

Other Opportunities in Electronics

The electronics industry offers a variety of career paths to people from all educational backgrounds. Here are just a few of the additional options not covered in detail in this book:

- Accountants and auditors
- Bookkeeping, accounting, and auditing clerks
- Computer and Internet security specialists
- Computer programmers
- Computer software engineers
- Computer systems analysts
- Customer service representatives
- Data entry and information processing workers
- Drafters
- Electrical and electronic equipment assemblers
- Industrial production managers
- Intellectual property lawyers
- Machinists
- Marketing and sales managers
- Network and computer systems administrators
- Office clerks
- Purchasing agents
- Receptionists
- Secretaries
- Security workers
- Web developers
- Webmasters

Military service is also an excellent method for beginning an electronics career. The military is one of the largest users of electronics technology and offers training and educational programs to enlisted personnel in many areas of electronics.

Finally, the rapid advancements in microelectronics may make it desirable or even necessary for you to continue to take courses, receive training, and study various trade journals throughout your career.

Certification or Licensing

Certification is not mandatory in most areas of electronics (although technicians working with radio-transmitting devices are required to be licensed by the Federal Communications Commission), but voluntary certification may prove useful in locating work and in increasing your pay and responsibilities. The International Society of Certified Electronics Technicians (ISCET) offers certification testing to technicians with four years of experience or schooling, as well as associate-level testing of basic electronics for beginning technicians. ISCET also offers a variety of study and training materials to help you prepare for the certification tests.

Other Requirements

Microelectronics technicians are involved in creating prototypes—that is, new and untested technology. This aspect of the field brings special responsibilities for carrying out assembly and testing procedures. These procedures must be performed with a high degree of precision. When assembling a new component, for example, you must be able to follow the design engineer's specifications and instructions exactly. Similar diligence and attention to detail are necessary when following the different procedures for testing the new components. An understanding of the underlying technology is important.

EXPLORING

You can begin exploring this field by getting involved in science clubs and working on electronics projects at home. Any part-time experience repairing electronic equipment will give you exposure to the basics of electronics.

You can find many resources for electronics experiments and projects in your school or local library or on the Internet. Summer employment in any type of electronics will be useful. Talking with someone who works in the field may help you narrow your focus to one particular area of electronics.

Microelectronics technicians assemble circuit boards for ISDN connections. *(Photothek.net/SV-Bilderdienst, The Image Works)*

EMPLOYERS

Many of the 170,000 electrical and electronics engineering technicians employed in the United States work in the computers, electronics, and communications fields. Because these fields are geographically concentrated in California, Texas, and Massachusetts, many electronics technician jobs are located in these areas. Positions are available elsewhere, but many technicians relocate to work in these focal areas. Some electronics technicians are self-employed, some work for large corporations, and others work in government-related jobs.

STARTING OUT

Most schools provide job placement services to students completing their degree program. Many offer on-the-job training as a part of the program. An internship or other real-life experience is desirable but not necessary. Many companies have extensive on-site training programs.

Newspapers and trade journals post openings for people working in electronics, and some companies recruit new hires directly on campus. Government employment offices are also good sources when looking for job leads.

ADVANCEMENT

Microelectronics technicians who choose to continue their education can expect to increase their responsibilities and be eligible to advance to supervisory and managerial positions.

Microelectronics technicians may also desire to enter other, more demanding areas of microelectronics, such as semiconductor development and engineering. Additional education may be necessary; engineers will be required to hold at least a four-year degree in electronics engineering.

Earning certification from the International Society of Certified Electronics Technicians may be part of the requirement for advancement in certain companies.

EARNINGS

According to the U.S. Department of Labor, median annual earnings of electrical and electronics engineering technicians were $52,140 in 2007. Salaries ranged from less than $31,310 to more than $75,910. Mean annual earnings of technicians who worked in the semiconductor and other electronic component manufacturing industry were $49,270 in 2007. Those in managerial or supervisory positions earn higher salaries, ranging between $55,000 and $85,000 per year. Wage rates vary greatly, according to skill level, type of employer, and location. Most employers offer some fringe benefits, including paid holidays and vacations, sick leave, and life and health insurance.

WORK ENVIRONMENT

Microelectronics technicians generally work a 40-hour week, although they may be assigned to different shifts or be required to work weekends and holidays. Overtime and holiday pay can usually be expected in such circumstances. The work setting is extremely clean, well lighted, and dust free.

Microelectronics technicians have many duties, and this requires them to be flexible yet focused as they perform their duties. They have to be exact and precise in their work no matter what they're doing, whether building an electronic component, running the tests, or recording the data. The fact that each day is often very different from the one before it is an aspect of the job that many technicians find appealing.

"One of the best things about the job is that it's always changing. We're always trying to make a better product, reduce cycle time, make it smaller or cheaper," says Kyle Turner. "You're always learning because it changes like crazy."

OUTLOOK

Jobs in the electronics industry are expected to grow more slowly than the average through 2016, according to the U.S. Department of Labor. The increasing reliability and durability of electronic technology will have some effect on the need for technicians. Similarly, increasing imports of microelectronics products, components, and technology may represent a decrease in production in this country, which will in turn decrease the numbers of microelectronics technicians needed here. Additionally, the use of advanced technologies, such as computer-aided design and drafting and computer simulation, will improve worker productivity and limit employment growth. Nevertheless, the government will continue to account for a large part of the demand for microelectronics components, technology, and personnel.

FOR MORE INFORMATION

For information on certification and student chapters, contact
International Society of Certified Electronics Technicians
3608 Pershing Avenue
Fort Worth, TX 76107-4527
Tel: 800-946-0201
Email: info@iscet.org
http://www.iscet.org

For information on semiconductors, a glossary of terms, and industry information, contact
Semiconductor Industry Association
181 Metro Drive, Suite 450
San Jose, CA 95110-1344
Tel: 408-436-6600
Email: mailbox@sia-online.org
http://www.sia-online.org

Quality Assurance Testers

OVERVIEW

Quality assurance testers examine new or modified computer software applications or computer hardware to evaluate whether they perform as intended. Testers might also verify that computer-automated quality assurance programs function properly. Their work entails trying to crash computer programs by punching in certain characters very quickly, for example, or by clicking the mouse on the border of an icon. They keep very close track of the combinations they enter so that they can replicate the situation if the program does crash. They also offer opinions on the user-friendliness of the program or the performance of hardware such as modems, hard drives, and printers. They report in detail any problems they find or suggestions they have both verbally and in writing to supervisors.

HISTORY

The first major advances in modern computer technology were made during World War II. After the war, it was thought that the enormous size of computers, which easily took up the space of entire warehouses, would limit their use to huge government projects. Accordingly, the 1950 census was computer processed.

The introduction of semiconductors to computer technology made possible smaller and less expensive computers. Businesses began adapting computers to their operations as early as 1954. Within 30 years, computers had revolutionized the way people work, play, and shop. Today, computers are everywhere, from businesses of all

QUICK FACTS

School Subjects
Computer science
Mathematics

Personal Skills
Mechanical/manipulative
Technical/scientific

Work Environment
Primarily indoors
Primarily one location

Minimum Education Level
High school diploma

Salary Range
$18,630 to $64,000 to $83,719+

Certification or Licensing
Voluntary

Outlook
Faster than the average

DOT
033

GOE
08.02.03

NOC
2233

O*NET-SOC
51-9061.00

kinds to government agencies, charitable organizations, and private homes. Over the years, the technology has continued to shrink computer size as their speeds have increased at an unprecedented rate.

Engineers have been able to significantly increase the memory capacity and processing speed of computer hardware. These technological advances enable computers to effectively process more information than ever before. Consequently, more sophisticated software applications have been created. These programs offer extremely user-friendly and sophisticated working environments that would not have been possible on older, slower computers. In addition, the introduction of CD-ROMs and DVD-ROMs to the mass computer market enabled the production of complex programs stored on compact discs.

As software applications became more complicated, the probability and sheer number of errors increased. Quality assurance departments were expanded to develop methods for testing software applications for errors, or "bugs." Quality assurance is now a branch of science and engineering in its own right. "Testing is finally being recognized as an important phase of the product cycle," says Steve Devinney, a senior consultant at the Quality Assurance Institute in Orlando, Florida. The importance of good testing procedures came to the forefront of the computer industry in the late 1990s with the emergence of the Year 2000 (Y2K) problems. "Testers were second-class citizens," says Devinney. "The thought was that if the project was running late, you could just skip the testing. Now, because of the Y2K situation, testing has become more important."

The field has changed with the advent of automated testing tools. As technology continues to advance, many quality assurance tests are automated. Quality assurance testers also "test the tests," that is, look for errors in the programs that test the software. There will always be a need for quality assurance testers, however, since they, not another computer, are best suited to judge a program from a user's point of view. "The use of tools will increase, but they can never replace humans," notes Devinney.

THE JOB

Before manufacturers can introduce a product on the consumer market, they must run extensive tests on its safety and quality. Failing to do so thoroughly can be very expensive, resulting in liability lawsuits when unsafe products harm people or in poor sales when products do not perform well. The nature and scope of quality assurance testing varies greatly. High-tech products, such as computers and other electronics, require extremely detailed technical testing.

Computer software applications undergo a specific series of tests designed to anticipate and help solve problems that users might encounter. Quality assurance testers examine new or modified computer software applications to evaluate whether they function at the desired level. They also verify that computer automated quality assurance programs perform in accordance with designer specifications and user requirements. This includes checking the product's functionality (how it will work), network performance (how it will work with other products), installation (how to put it in), and configuration (how it is set up).

Some quality assurance testers spend most of their time working on software programs or playing computer games, just as an average consumer might. If it is a game, for example, they play it over and over again for hours, trying to make moves quickly or slowly to "crash" it. A program crashes if it completely stops functioning due to, among other things, an inability to process incoming commands. For other types of programs, such as word processors, quality assurance testers might intentionally make errors, type very quickly, or click the mouse on inappropriate areas of the screen to see if the program can correctly handle such usage.

Quality assurance testers keep detailed records of the hours logged working on individual programs. They write reports based on their observations about how well the program performed in different situations, always imagining how typical, nontechnical users would judge it. The goal is to make the programs more efficient, user-friendly, fun, and visually exciting. Lastly, they keep track of the precise combinations of keystrokes and mouse clicks that made the program crash. This type of record is very important because it enables supervisors and programmers to replicate the problem. Then they can better isolate its source and begin to design a solution.

Programs to be tested arrive in the quality assurance department after programmers and software engineers have finished the initial version. Each program is assigned a specific number of tests, and the quality assurance testers go to work. They make sure that the correct tests are run, write reports, and send the program back to the programmers for revisions and correction. Some testers have direct contact with the programmers. After evaluating a product, they might meet with programmers to describe the problems they encountered and suggest ways for solving glitches. Others report solely to a quality assurance supervisor.

When automated tests are to be run, quality assurance testers tell the computer which tests to administer and then ensure that they run smoothly by watching a computer screen for interruption codes and breakdown signals. They also interpret test results, verifying their credibility by running them through special programs that check for accuracy and reliability. Then, they write reports explaining their conclusions.

Some quality assurance testers have direct contact with users experiencing problems with their software. They listen closely to customer complaints to determine the precise order of keystrokes that led to the problem. Then, they attempt to duplicate the problem on their own computers and run in-depth tests to figure out the cause. Eventually, if the problem is not simply a result of user error, they inform programmers and software engineers of the problems and suggest certain paths to take in resolving them.

Quality assurance testers with solid work experience and bachelor's degrees in a computer-related field might go on to work as *quality assurance analysts*. Analysts write and revise the quality standards for each software program that passes through the department. They also use computer programming skills to create the tests and programs the quality assurance testers use to test the programs. They might evaluate proposals for new software applications, advising management about whether the program will be able to achieve its goals. Since they know many software applications inside and out, they might also train users on how to work with various programs.

REQUIREMENTS

High School

Interested in becoming a quality assurance tester? If so, then take as many computer classes as possible to become familiar with how to effectively operate computer software and hardware. Math and science courses are very helpful for teaching the necessary analytical skills. English and speech classes will help you improve your verbal and written communications skills, which are also essential to the success of quality assurance testers.

Postsecondary Training

It is debatable whether a bachelor's degree is necessary to become a quality assurance tester. Some companies require a bachelor's degree in computer science, while others prefer people who come from the business sector who have a small amount of computer experience because they best match the technical level of the software's typical users. If testers are interested in advancement, however, a bachelor's degree is almost a mandate.

Few universities or colleges offer courses on quality assurance testing. As a result, most companies offer in-house training on how to test their particular products.

Certification or Licensing

As the information technology industry becomes more competitive, the necessity for management to be able to distinguish professional and skilled individuals in the field becomes mandatory, according to the Quality Assurance Institute. Certification demonstrates a level of understanding in carrying out relevant principles and practices, and provides a common ground for communication among professionals in the field of software quality. The organization offers the designations certified software tester, certified software quality analyst, certified software project manager, certified manager of software testing, and certified manager of software quality.

Other Requirements

Quality assurance testers need superior verbal and written communications skills. They also must show a proficiency in critical and analytical thinking and be able to critique something diplomatically. Quality assurance testers should have an eye for detail, be focused, and have a lot of enthusiasm because sometimes the work is monotonous and repetitive. Testers should definitely enjoy the challenge of breaking the system.

Some companies recommend testers have some programming skills in languages such as C, C++, SQL, or Visual Basic. Others prefer testers with no programming ability. "The most important thing is that testers understand the business and the testing tools with which they are working," says Steve Devinney. "You have to be a good problem-solver and detective. Testing is a difficult job."

EXPLORING

Students interested in quality assurance and other computer jobs should gain wide exposure to computer systems and programs of all kinds. Get a computer at home, borrow a friend's, or check out the computer lab at your school. Work on becoming comfortable using the Windows programs and learn how to operate all parts of your computer, including the hardware, thoroughly. Look for bugs in your software at home and practice writing them up. Keep up with emerging technologies. If you cannot get hands-on experiences, read about them. Join a computer group or society. Read books on testing and familiarize yourself with methodology, terminology, the development cycle, and where testing fits in. Subscribe to newsletters or magazines that are related to testing or quality assurance. Get involved with online newsgroups that deal with the subject. Check Web sites that deal with quality assurance.

If you live in an area where numerous computer software companies are located, you might be able to secure a part-time or summer job as a quality assurance tester. In addition, investigate the possibility of spending an afternoon with an employed quality assurance tester to find out what a typical day is like for him or her.

EMPLOYERS

Quality assurance testers are employed throughout the United States. Opportunities are best in large cities and suburbs where business and industry are active. Many work for electronics and software manufacturers, a cluster of which are located in Silicon Valley, in northern California. There are also concentrations of software manufacturers in Boston, Chicago, and Atlanta.

STARTING OUT

Positions in the field of quality assurance can be obtained several different ways. Many universities and colleges host computer job fairs on campus throughout the year that include representatives from several hardware and software companies. Internships and summer jobs with such corporations are always beneficial and provide experience that will give you the edge over your competition. General computer job fairs are also held throughout the year in larger cities. Some job openings are advertised in newspapers. There are many career sites on the Web that post job openings, salary surveys, and current employment trends. The Web also has online publications that deal specifically with quality assurance. You can also obtain information from associations for quality professionals, such as the Quality Assurance Institute, and from computer organizations, including the IEEE Computer Society.

ADVANCEMENT

Quality assurance testers are considered entry-level positions in some companies. After acquiring more experience and technical knowledge, testers might become quality assurance analysts, who write and revise the quality assurance standards or specifications for new programs. They also create the quality assurance examinations that testers use to evaluate programs. This usually involves using computer programming. Some analysts also evaluate proposals for new software products to decide whether the proposed product is capable of doing what it is supposed to do. Analysts are sometimes promoted to quality assurance manager positions, which require some knowledge of software coding, the entire software production process, and test automation. They manage quality assurance teams for specific software products before and beyond their release.

Some testers also go on to become programmers or software engineers.

EARNINGS

Software quality assurance testers earned salaries that ranged from less than $44,042 to $84,581 or more annually in 2008, according to Salary.com. Workers with many years of technical and management experience can earn higher salaries. Testers in all industries had earnings that ranged from less than $18,630 to $52,230 or more annually in 2007, according to the U.S. Department of Labor. Those employed in semiconductor and other electronic component manufacturing had mean annual earnings of $31,030. Testers generally receive a full benefits package as well, including health insurance, paid vacation, and sick leave. As in many industries, people with advanced degrees have the potential to make the most money.

WORK ENVIRONMENT

Quality assurance testers work in computer labs or offices. The work is generally repetitive and even monotonous. If a game is being tested, for example, a tester may have to play it for hours until it finally crashes, if at all. This might seem like great fun, but most testers agree that even the newest, most exciting game loses its appeal after several hours. This aspect of the job proves to be very frustrating and boring for some individuals.

Since quality assurance work involves keeping very detailed records, the job can also be stressful. For example, if a tester works on a word processing program for several hours, he or she must be able to recall at any moment the last few keystrokes entered in case the program crashes. This requires long periods of concentration, which can be tiring. Monitoring computer screens to make sure automated quality assurance tests are running properly often has the same effect.

Meeting with supervisors, programmers, and engineers to discuss ideas for the software projects can be intellectually stimulating. At these times, testers should feel at ease communicating with superiors. On the other end, testers who field customer complaints on the telephone may be forced to bear the brunt of customer dissatisfaction, an almost certain source of stress.

Quality assurance testers generally work regular, 40-hour weeks. During the final stages before a program goes into mass production and packaging, however, testers are frequently called on to work overtime.

OUTLOOK

Employment for quality assurance testers is expected to grow faster than the average for all occupations over the next decade. This trend is predicted despite an increasing level of quality assurance automation. Before, software companies were able to make big profits by being the first to introduce a specific kind of product, such as a word processor or presentation kit, to the marketplace. Now, with so many versions of similar software on the market, competition is forcing firms to focus their energies on customer service. Many companies, therefore, aim to perfect their software applications before they hit the shelves. Searching for every small program glitch in this way requires the effort of many quality assurance testers.

This same push toward premarket perfection helps to explain the development of more accurate and efficient quality assurance automation. To stay competitive, companies must refine their quality assurance procedures to ever-higher levels. "In the next few years, testing will begin on Day One of the project," says Steve Devinney. "This means that testers will be involved in the process from the beginning because they are the ones who know what the product's functionality should be. Without testing requirements, you cannot do anything."

FOR MORE INFORMATION

For information on scholarships, student membership, and to read Careers in Computer Science and Computer Engineering, *visit the IEEE Web site.*

IEEE Computer Society
2001 L Street NW, Suite 700
Washington, DC 20036-4910
Tel: 202-371-0101
http://www.computer.org

For career advice and industry information, contact
International Game Developers Association
19 Mantua Road
Mt. Royal, NJ 08061-1006

Tel: 856-423-2990
Email: contact@igda.org
http://www.igda.org

For information on certification, contact
Quality Assurance Institute
2101 Park Center Drive, Suite 200
Orlando, FL 32835-7614
Tel: 407-363-1111
Email: qaiadmin@qaiusa.com
http://www.qaiworldwide.org

For industry information, contact the following organizations:
Software & Information Industry Association
1090 Vermont Avenue, NW, Sixth Floor
Washington, DC 20005-4095
Tel: 202-289-7442
http://www.siia.net

Software Testing Institute
http://www.softwaretestinginstitute.com

Semiconductor Technicians

OVERVIEW

Semiconductor technicians are highly skilled workers who test new kinds of semiconductor devices being designed for use in many kinds of modern electronic equipment. They may also test samples of devices already in production to assess production techniques. They help develop and evaluate the test equipment used to gather information about the semiconductor devices. Working under the direction provided by engineers in research laboratory settings, they assist in the design and planning for later production or help to improve production yields. Approximately 42,000 semiconductor technicians are employed in the United States.

HISTORY

Semiconductors and devices utilizing them are found in nearly every electronic product made today, from complicated weapons systems and space technology to personal computers, digital video disc players, cellular telephones, and programmable coffeemakers. The manufacturing of semiconductors and microelectronics devices requires the efforts of a variety of people, from the engineers who design them, to the technicians who process, construct, and test them.

Although the word semiconductor is often used to refer to microchips or integrated circuits, a semiconductor is actually the basic material of these devices. Semiconductor materials are so called because they can be switched to act with properties between that of an insulator, which does not conduct electrical current, and that of a true conductor of electrical current, such as metal.

Silicon is the most common material used as a semiconductor. Other semiconductor materials may be gallium arsenide, cadmium sulfide, and selenium sulfide. Doping, or treating, these materials with substances such as aluminum, arsenic, boron, and phosphorous gives them conducting properties. By applying these substances according to a specifically designed layout, engineers and technicians construct the tiny electronic devices—transistors, capacitors, and resistors—of an integrated circuit. A microchip no larger than a fingernail may contain many thousands of these devices.

THE JOB

There are many steps that occur in processing semiconductors into integrated circuits. The technicians involved in these processes are called *semiconductor development technicians* and *semiconductor process technicians*. They may be involved in several or many of the steps of semiconductor manufacturing, depending on where they work. Often, semiconductor technicians function as a link between the engineering staff and the production staff in the large-scale manufacturing of semiconductor products.

The making of semiconductors begins with silicon. The silicon must be extremely pure to be of use. The silicon used for semiconductors is heated in a furnace and formed into cylinder rods between one and six inches in diameter and three or more feet in length. These rods are smoothed and polished until they are perfectly round. They are then sliced into wafers that are between one-quarter and one-half millimeter in thickness. Then the wafers are processed, by etching, polishing, heat-treating, and lapping, to produce the desired dimensions and surface finish. After the wafers are tested, measured, and inspected for any defects, they are coated with a photosensitive substance called a photoresist.

The engineering staff and the technicians assigned to assist them prepare designs for the layout of the microchip. This work is generally done using a computer-aided design (CAD) system. The large, completed design is then miniaturized as a photomask when it is applied to the wafer. The photomask is placed over the wafer and the photoresist is developed, much like film in a camera, with ultraviolet light, so that the layout of the microchip is reproduced many times on the same wafer. This work takes place in a specially equipped clean room, or laboratory, that is kept completely free of

An Intel semiconductor technician produces chips in a clean room. *(Paul Sakuma, AP Photo)*

dust and other impurities. During the miniaturization process, the tiniest speck of dust will ruin the reproduction of the layout onto the wafer.

Next, the wafer is doped with the substances that will give it the necessary conducting properties. Technicians follow the layout, like a road map, when adding these substances. The proper combinations of materials create the various components of the integrated circuit. When this process is complete, the wafer is tested by computerized equipment that can test the many thousands of components in a matter of seconds. Many of the integrated circuits on the wafer will not function properly, and these are marked and discarded. After testing, the wafer is cut up into its individual chips.

The chips are then packaged by placing them in a casing usually made of plastic or ceramic, which also contains metal leads for connecting the microchip into the electronic circuitry of the device for which it will be used. It is this package that is usually referred to as a chip or semiconductor.

Semiconductor process technicians are generally responsible for the fabrication and processing of the semiconductor wafer. *Semiconductor development technicians* usually assist with the basic design and development of rough sketches of a prototype chip; they may be involved in transferring the layout to the wafer and in assembling and testing the semiconductor. Both types of technicians gather and evaluate data on the semiconductor, wafer, or chip. They are responsible for ensuring that each step of the process precisely meets test specifications, and also for identifying flaws and problems in the material and design. Technicians may also assist in designing and building new test equipment, and in communicating test data and production instructions for large-scale manufacture. Technicians may also be responsible for maintaining the equipment and for training operators on its use.

REQUIREMENTS

The nature of the microelectronics industry, in which technological advances are continuous and rapid, means that some form of higher education, whether in a two-year or four-year program, is a must. An early interest in and excitement for electronics and computers is a good indicator of someone who might be interested in this career.

High School
Math and science courses, as well as classes in computers and computer science, are requirements for students wishing to enter the semiconductor and microelectronics field. Physics and chemistry will help you understand many of the processes involved in developing and fabricating semiconductors and semiconductor components. Strong communications skills are also very important.

Postsecondary Training
Technician jobs in microelectronics and semiconductor technology require at least an associate's degree in electronics or electrical engineering or technology. Students may attend a two-year program at a community college or vocational school. Students interested in a career at the engineering level should consider studying for a bachelor's degree. The trend toward greater specialization within the industry may make a bachelor's degree more desirable over an associate's degree in the future.

An electronics engineering program will include courses in electronics theory, as well as math, science, and English. Students can expect to study such subjects as the principle and models of semiconductor devices; physics for solid-state electronics; solid-state theory; introduction to VLSI systems; and basic courses in computer organization, electromagnetic fundamentals, digital and analog laboratories, and the design of circuits and active networks. Companies will also provide additional training on the specific equipment and software they use. Many companies also offer training programs and educational opportunities to employees to increase their skills and their responsibilities.

Courses are available at many community and junior colleges, which may be more flexible in their curriculum and better able to keep up with technological advances than vocational training schools. The latter, however, will often have programs geared specifically to the needs of the employers in their area and may have job placement programs and relationships with the different companies available as well. If you are interested in these schools, you should do some research to determine whether the training offered is thorough and that the school has a good placement record. Training institutes should also be accredited by the Accrediting Commission of Career Schools and Colleges of Technology (http://www.accsct.org).

Military service may also provide a strong background in electronics. In addition, the tuition credits available to military personnel will be helpful when continuing your education.

Certification or Licensing
Certification is not mandatory, but voluntary certification may prove useful in locating work and in increasing your pay and responsibilities. The International Society of Certified Electronics Technicians (ISCET) offers certification testing at various levels and fields of electronics. The ISCET also offers a variety of study and training material to help prepare for the certification tests.

Other Requirements
A thorough understanding of semiconductors, electronics, and the production process is necessary for semiconductor technicians. Investigative and research skills, and a basic knowledge of computers and computer programs are important for the prospective semiconductor technician. "You have to be very patient and not easily discouraged to work in this industry," says Jan Gilliam, a semiconductor technician at Advanced Micro Devices, located in Austin, Texas. "You have to really focus on the goal while paying close attention to details."

EXPLORING

You can develop your interests in computers and microelectronics while in school. Most high schools will be unable to keep up with the rapid advances in electronics technology, and you will need to read and explore on your own. Joining extracurricular clubs in computers or electronics will give you an opportunity for hands-on learning experiences.

Facts About the U.S. Semiconductor Industry

- Approximately 233,000 workers are employed in the semiconductor industry.
- Industry sales reached $118 billion in 2007.
- The industry had a 46 percent world market share in 2007.
- Employment in semiconductor manufacturing is expected to decline by 13.7 percent through 2016.

Sources: U.S. Department of Labor, Semiconductor Industry Association

You should also begin to seek out the higher education appropriate for your future career interests. Your high school guidance counselor should be able to help you find a training program that will match your career goals.

EMPLOYERS

Approximately 42,000 semiconductor technicians are employed in the United States. Finding a job in the semiconductor industry may mean living in the right part of the country. Certain states, such as California, Texas, and Massachusetts, have many more opportunities than others. Some of the big names in semiconductors include Intel, Motorola, Texas Instruments, and National Semiconductor. These companies are very large and employ many technicians, but there are smaller and mid-size companies in the industry as well.

STARTING OUT

Semiconductor technician positions can be located through the career services office of a community college or vocational training school. Since an associate's degree is recommended, many of these degree programs provide students with job interviews and introductions to companies in the community that are looking for qualified workers.

Job listings in newspapers or at local employment agencies are also good places for locating job opportunities. Aspiring semiconductor technicians can also find less-skilled positions in the semiconductor industry and work hard for promotion to a technician position. Having more education and training will give you an advantage in the huge job market for semiconductors and related devices.

ADVANCEMENT

As with any manufacturing industry, the advancement possibilities available to semiconductor technicians will depend on their levels of skill, education, and experience. Technicians may advance to *senior technicians* or may find themselves in supervisory or management positions. Technicians with two-year associate's degrees may elect to continue their education. Often, their course work will be transferable to a four-year engineering program, and many times their employer may help pay for their continuing education. Semiconductor technicians may ultimately choose to enter the engineering and design areas of the field. Also, a background in semiconductor processing and development may lead to a career in sales or purchasing of semiconductor components, materials, and equipment.

EARNINGS

Semiconductor technicians earned a median hourly wage of $15.32, or $31,870 a year, in 2007, according to the U.S. Department of Labor. Ten percent of all workers earned less than $10.40 an hour ($21,630 a year), while the top 10 percent earned $24.68 or more an hour ($51,330 a year). Technicians earning higher salaries have more education or have worked in the industry for many years.

Benefits for semiconductor technicians depend on the employer; however, they usually include such items as health insurance, retirement or 401(k) plans, and paid vacation days.

WORK ENVIRONMENT

The work of semiconductor technicians is not physically strenuous and is usually done in an extremely clean environment. Technicians may work with hazardous chemicals, however, and proper safety precautions must be strictly followed. Because of the large demand for semiconductors and related devices, many facilities, like Advanced Micro Devices, where Jan Gilliam works, operate with two 12-hour shifts, meaning that a technician may be assigned to the night or weekend shift, or on a rotating schedule. Gilliam works for three days and then is off for four.

Because of the need for an extremely clean environment, technicians are required to wear clean-suits to keep dust, lint, and dirt out of the clean room where the production takes place.

An important component in most manufacturing processes is the speed with which products are produced. Workers may find themselves under a great deal of pressure to maintain a certain level of production volume. The ability to work well in a sometimes stressful environment is an important quality for any prospective semiconductor technician.

OUTLOOK

The U.S. Department of Labor predicts a decline in employment in the semiconductor industry through 2016. This decline is due to two main factors: higher productivity and increased imports. Many semiconductor manufacturers have installed new machinery that can produce twice as many wafers as the old machines. This increased automation has streamlined the staff of many manufacturing plants. Also, manufacturers have begun to build plants in overseas locations where semiconductors can be made more cheaply than in the United States. In addition, imports of more affordable semiconductors from non-U.S. manufacturers is expected to rise in the coming years, which will lessen the need for semiconductor manufacturing technicians in the United States.

Despite this decline, semiconductors will be in greater demand than ever before, due to the increasing number of electronics and computers that use them. For example, the new 64-bit microchip, which provides desktop computers with greater power and memory, will lead to the development of many new electronic products, especially in the medical industry. Technicians will be needed to build the components for new products, as well as to replace the many technicians who will be reaching retirement age. Jobs will go to the technicians with the most education, training, and technical experience.

FOR MORE INFORMATION

For certification information, contact
   International Society of Certified Electronics Technicians
   3608 Pershing Avenue
   Fort Worth, TX 76107-4527
   Tel: 817-921-9101
   Email: info@iscet.org
   http://www.iscet.org

For industry information, contact
   Semiconductor Equipment and Materials International
   3081 Zanker Road
   San Jose, CA 95134-2127
   Tel: 408-943-6900
   Email: semihq@semi.org
   http://www.semi.org

For information on semiconductors, a glossary of terms, and industry information, contact

Semiconductor Industry Association
181 Metro Drive, Suite 450
San Jose, CA 95110-1344
Tel: 408-436-6600
Email: mailbox@sia-online.org
http://www.sia-online.org

Technical Writers and Editors

OVERVIEW

Technical writers, sometimes called *technical communicators*, express technical and scientific ideas in easy-to-understand language. *Technical editors* revise written text to correct any errors and make it read smoothly and clearly. They also may coordinate the activities of technical writers, technical illustrators, and other staff in preparing material for publication and oversee the document development and production processes. Technical writers hold about 49,000 jobs in the United States. Editors of all types (including technical editors) hold 122,000 jobs.

HISTORY

Humans have used writing to communicate information for more than 5,500 years. Technical writing, though, did not emerge as a specific profession in the United States until the early years of the 20th century. Before that time, engineers, scientists, and researchers did any necessary writing themselves.

During the early 1900s, technology expanded rapidly. The use of machines to manufacture and mass-produce a wide number of products paved the way for more complex and technical products. Scientists and researchers were discovering new technologies and applications for technology, particularly in electronics, medicine, and engineering. The need to record studies and research, and report them to others, grew. Also,

QUICK FACTS

School Subjects
Business
English

Personal Skills
Communication/ideas
Technical/scientific

Work Environment
Primarily indoors
Primarily one location

Minimum Education Level
Bachelor's degree

Salary Range
$36,490 to $60,390 to
   $94,550+ (writers)
$27,360 to $48,320 to
   $91,390+ (editors)

Certification or Licensing
None available

Outlook
Faster than the average
   (writers)
Little or no change (editors)

DOT
131 (writers)
132 (editors)

GOE
01.02.01

NOC
5121 (writers)
5122 (editors)

O*NET-SOC
27-3042.00, 27-3043.00
   (writers)
27-3041.00 (editors)

as products became more complex, it was necessary to provide information that documented their components, showed how they were assembled, and explained how to install, use, and repair them. By the mid-1920s, writers were being used to help engineers and scientists document their work and prepare technical information for nontechnical audiences.

Editors have worked with printers and authors for many years. They check copies of a printed document to correct any errors made during printing, to rewrite unclear passages, and to correct errors in spelling, grammar, and punctuation. As the need for technical writers grew, so too did the need for technical editors. Editors became more involved in documents before the printing stage, and today work closely with writers as they prepare their materials. Many editors coordinate the activities of all the people involved in preparing technical communications and manage the document development and production processes.

The need for technical writers grew further with the growth of the computer industry beginning in the 1960s. Originally, many computer companies used computer programmers to write user manuals and other documentation. It was widely assumed that the material was so complex that only those who were involved with creating computer programs would be able to write about them. Although computer programmers had the technical knowledge, many were not able to write clear, easy-to-use manuals. Complaints about the difficulty of using and understanding manuals were common. By the 1970s, computer companies began to hire technical writers to write computer manuals and documents. Today, this is one of the largest areas in which technical writers are employed.

The need for technical marketing writers also grew as a result of expanding computer technology. Many copywriters who worked for advertising agencies and marketing firms did not have the technical background to be able to describe the features of the technical products that were coming to market. Thus developed the need for writers who could combine the ability to promote products with the ability to communicate technical information.

The nature of technical writers' and technical editors' jobs continues to change with emerging technologies. Today, the ability to store, transmit, and receive information through computers and electronic means is changing the very nature of documents. Traditional books and paper documents are being replaced by CD-ROMs, interactive multimedia documents, and material accessed through bulletin board systems, faxes, the World Wide Web, and the Internet.

THE JOB

Technical writers and editors prepare a wide variety of documents and materials. The most common types of documents they produce are manuals, technical reports, specifications, and proposals. Some technical writers also write scripts for videos and audiovisual presentations and text for multimedia programs. Technical writers and editors prepare manuals that give instructions and detailed information on how to install, assemble, use, service, or repair a product or equipment. They may write and edit manuals as simple as a two-page leaflet that gives instructions on how to program a cordless phone or as complex as a 500-page document that tells service technicians how to repair machinery, medical equipment, or a climate-control system. One of the most common types of manuals is the computer software manual, which informs users on how to load software on their computers, explains how to use the program, and gives information on different features.

Technical writers and editors also prepare technical reports on a multitude of subjects. These reports include documents that give the results of research and laboratory tests and documents that describe the progress of a project (for example, the development of a faster computer chip). They also write and edit sales proposals, product specifications, quality standards, journal articles, in-house style manuals, and newsletters.

The work of a technical writer begins when he or she is assigned to prepare a document. The writer meets with members of an account or technical team to learn the requirements for the document, the intended purpose or objectives, and the audience. During the planning stage, the writer learns when the document needs to be completed, approximately how long it should be, whether artwork or illustrations are to be included, who the other team members are, and any other production or printing requirements. A schedule is created that defines the different stages of development and determines when the writer needs to have certain parts of the document ready.

The next step in document development is the research, or information gathering, phase. During this stage, technical writers gather all the available information about the product or subject, read and review it, and determine what other information is needed. They may research the topic by reading technical publications, but in most cases they will need to gather information directly from the people working on the product. Writers meet with and interview people who are sources of information, such as scientists, engineers, software developers, computer programmers, managers, and project managers. They ask questions, listen, and take notes or record interviews. They gather any available notes, drawings, or diagrams that may be useful.

After writers gather all the necessary information, they sort it out and organize it. They plan how they are going to present the information and prepare an outline for the document. They may decide how the document will look and prepare the design, format, and layout of the pages. In some cases, this may be done by an editor rather than the writer. If illustrations, diagrams, or photographs are going to be included, either the editor or writer makes arrangements for an illustrator, photographer, or art researcher to produce or obtain them.

Then, the writer starts writing and prepares a rough draft of the document. If the document is very large, a writer may prepare it in segments. Once the rough draft is completed, it is submitted to a designated person or group for technical review. Copies of the draft are distributed to managers, engineers, or other experts who can easily determine if any technical information is inaccurate or missing. These reviewers read the document and suggest changes.

The rough draft is also given to technical editors for review of a variety of factors. The editors check that the material is organized well, that each section flows with the section before and after it, and that the language is appropriate for the intended audience (scientists, engineers, a company's CEO, or board of directors, etc.). They also check for correct use of grammar, spelling, and punctuation. They ensure that names of parts or objects are consistent throughout the document and that references are accurate. They also check the labeling of graphs and captions for accuracy. Technical editors use special symbols, called proofreader's marks, to indicate the types of changes needed.

The editor and reviewers return their copies of the document to the technical writer. The writer incorporates the appropriate suggestions and revisions and prepares the final draft. The final draft is once again submitted to a designated reviewer or team of reviewers. In some cases, the technical reviewer may do a quick check to make sure that the requested changes were made. In other cases, the technical reviewer may examine the document in depth to ensure technical accuracy and correctness. A walkthrough, or test of the document, may be done for certain types of documents. For example, a walkthrough may be done for a document that explains how to assemble a product. A tester assembles the product by following the instructions given in the document. The tester makes a note of all sections that are unclear or inaccurate, and the document is returned to the writer for any necessary revisions.

Once the final draft has been approved, the document is submitted to the technical editor, who makes a comprehensive check of the document. In addition to checking that the language is clear and reads smoothly, the editor ensures that the table of contents matches the different sections or chapters of a document, all illustrations and diagrams are correctly placed, all captions are matched to the correct picture, consistent terminology is used, and correct references are used in the bibliography and text.

The editor returns the document to either the *writer* or a *word processor*, who makes any necessary corrections. This copy is then checked by a *proofreader*. The proofreader compares the final copy against the editor's marked-up copy and makes sure that all changes were made. The document is then prepared for printing. In some cases, the writer is responsible for preparing camera-ready copy or electronic files for printing purposes, and in other cases, a print production coordinator prepares all material to submit to a printer.

Some technical writers specialize in a specific type of material. *Technical marketing writers* create promotional and marketing materials for technological products. They may write the copy for an advertisement for a technical product, such as a cell phone, computer workstation, or software, or they may write press releases about the product. They also write sales literature, product flyers, Web pages, and multimedia presentations.

Other technical writers prepare scripts for videotapes, DVDs, and films about technical subjects. These writers, called *scriptwriters*, need to have an understanding of film and video production techniques.

Some technical writers and editors prepare articles for scientific, medical, computer, or engineering trade journals. These articles may report the results of research conducted by doctors, scientists, or engineers or report on technological advances in a particular field. Some technical writers and editors also develop textbooks. They may receive articles written by engineers or scientists and edit and revise them to make them more suitable for the intended audience.

Technical writers and editors may create documents for a variety of media. Electronic media, such as compact discs and online services, are increasingly being used in place of books and paper documents. Technical writers may create materials that are accessed through bulletin board systems and the Internet or create computer-based resources, such as help menus on computer programs. They also create interactive, multimedia documents that are distributed on compact discs. Some of these media require knowledge of special computer programs that allow material to be hyperlinked, or electronically cross-referenced.

REQUIREMENTS

High School

In high school, you should take composition, grammar, literature, creative writing, journalism, social studies, math, statistics, engineering, computer science, and as many science classes as possible. Business courses are also useful as they explain the organizational structure of companies and how they operate.

Postsecondary Training

Most employers prefer to hire technical writers and editors who have a bachelor's or advanced degree. Many technical editors graduate with degrees in the humanities, especially English or journalism. Technical writers typically need to have a strong foundation in engineering, computers, or science. Those employed in the electronics industry often have a degree in electrical or computer engineering or a related field. Many technical writers graduate with a degree in engineering or science and take classes in technical writing.

Many different types of college programs are available that prepare people to become technical writers and editors. A growing number of colleges are offering degrees in technical writing. Schools without a technical writing program may offer degrees in journalism or English. Programs are offered through English, communications, and journalism departments. Classes vary based on the type of program. In general, classes for technical writers include a core curriculum in writing and classes in algebra, statistics, logic, science, engineering, and computer programming languages. Useful classes for editors include technical writing, project management, grammar, proofreading, copyediting, and print production.

Many technical writers and editors earn a master's degree. In these programs, they study technical writing in depth and may specialize in a certain area, such as scriptwriting, instructional design, or multimedia applications. In addition, many nondegree writing programs are offered to technical writers and editors to hone their skills. Offered as extension courses or continuing education courses, these programs include courses on indexing, editing medical materials, writing for trade journals, and other related subjects.

Technical writers, and occasionally technical editors, are often asked to present samples of their work. College students should build a portfolio during their college years in which they collect their best samples from work that they may have done for a literary magazine, newsletter, or yearbook.

Technical writers and editors should be willing to pursue learning throughout their careers. As technology changes, technical writers and editors may need to take classes to update their knowledge. Changes in electronic printing and computer technology will also change the way technical writers and editors do their jobs, and writers and editors may need to take courses to learn new skills or new technologies.

Other Requirements

Technical writers need to have good communications skills, science and technical aptitudes, and the ability to think analytically. Technical editors also need to have good communications skills, and judgment, as well as the ability to identify and correct errors in written material. They need to be diplomatic, assertive, and able to explain tactfully what needs to be corrected to writers, engineers, and other people involved with a document. Technical editors should be able to understand technical information easily, but they need less scientific and technical background than writers. Both technical writers and editors need to be able to work as part of a team and collaborate with others on a project. They need to be highly self-motivated, well organized, and able to work under pressure.

EXPLORING

If you enjoy writing and are considering a career in technical writing or editing, you should make writing a daily activity. Writing is a skill that develops over time and through practice. You can keep journals, join writing clubs, and practice different types of writing, such as scriptwriting and informative reports. Sharing writing with others and asking them to critique it is especially helpful. Comments from readers on what they enjoyed about a piece of writing or difficulty they had in understanding certain sections provides valuable feedback that helps to improve your writing style.

Reading a variety of materials is also helpful. Reading exposes you to both good and bad writing styles and techniques, and helps you to identify why one approach works better than another.

You may also gain experience by working on a literary magazine, student newspaper, or yearbook (or starting one of your own if one is not available). Both writing and editing articles and managing production give you the opportunity to learn new skills and to see what is involved in preparing documents and other materials.

You may also be able to get internships, cooperative education assignments, or summer or part-time jobs as proofreaders or editorial assistants that may include writing responsibilities.

EMPLOYERS

There are approximately 49,000 technical writers currently employed in the United States. Editors of all types (including technical editors) hold 122,000 jobs.

Employment may be found in many different types of places, such as in the fields of electronics, aerospace, computers, engineering, pharmaceuticals, and research and development, or with the nuclear industry, medical publishers, government agencies or contractors, and colleges and universities. The aerospace, engineering, medical, and computer industries hire significant numbers of technical writers and editors. The federal government, particularly the Departments of Defense and Agriculture, the National Aeronautics and Space Administration, and the Nuclear Regulatory Commission, also hires many writers and editors with technical knowledge.

STARTING OUT

Many technical writers start their careers as scientists, engineers, technicians, or research assistants and move into writing after several years of experience in those positions. Technical writers with a bachelor's degree in a technical subject such as engineering may be able to find work as a technical writer immediately upon graduating from college, but many employers prefer to hire writers with some work experience.

Technical editors who graduate with a bachelor's degree in English or journalism may find entry-level work as *editorial assistants*, *copy editors*, or *proofreaders*. From these positions they are able to move into technical editing positions. Or beginning workers may find jobs as technical editors in small companies or those with a small technical communications department.

If you plan to work for the federal government, you need to pass an examination. Information about examinations and job openings is available at federal employment centers.

You may learn about job openings through your college's career services office and want ads in newspapers and professional magazines. You may also research companies that hire technical writers and editors and apply directly to them. Many libraries provide useful job resource guides and directories that provide information about companies that hire in specific areas.

ADVANCEMENT

As technical writers and editors gain experience, they move into more challenging and responsible positions. At first, they may work on simple documents or are assigned to work on sections of a document. As they demonstrate their proficiency and skills, they are given more complex assignments and are responsible for more activities.

Technical writers and editors with several years of experience may move into project management positions. As project managers, they are responsible for the entire document development and production processes. They schedule and budget resources and assign writers, editors, illustrators, and other workers to a project. They monitor the schedule, supervise workers, and ensure that costs remain in budget.

Technical writers and editors who show good project management skills, leadership abilities, and good interpersonal skills may become supervisors or managers. Both technical writers and editors can move into senior writer and senior editor positions. These positions involve increased responsibilities and may include supervising other workers.

Many technical writers and editors seek to develop and perfect their skills rather than move into management or supervisory positions. As they gain a reputation for their quality of work, they may be able to select choice assignments. They may learn new skills as a means of being able to work in new areas. For example, a technical writer may learn a new desktop program in order to become more proficient in designing. Or, a technical writer may learn a hypermedia or hypertext computer program in order to be able to create a multimedia program. Technical writers and editors who broaden their skill base and capabilities can move to higher-paying positions within their own company or at another company. They also may work as freelancers or set up their own communications companies.

EARNINGS

Median annual earnings for salaried technical writers were $60,390 in 2007, according to the U.S. Department of Labor (USDL). Salaries ranged from less than $36,490 to more than $94,550. The USDL reports the following mean salaries for technical writers by industry: software publishers, $70,380; computer systems design and related services, $66,090; management, scientific, and technical consulting services, $64,000; and architectural, engineering, and related services, $59,530.

Editors of all types earned a median salary of $48,320 in 2007. The lowest paid 10 percent earned $27,360 or less and the highest paid 10 percent earned $91,390 or more.

Most companies offer benefits that include paid holidays and vacations, medical insurance, and 401(k) plans. They may also offer profit sharing, pension plans, and tuition assistance programs.

WORK ENVIRONMENT

Technical writers and editors usually work in an office environment, with well-lit and quiet surroundings. They may have their own offices or share workspace with other writers and editors. Most writers and editors have computers. They may be able to utilize the services of support staff who can word-process revisions, run off copies, fax material, and perform other administrative functions or they may have to perform all of these tasks themselves.

Some technical writers and editors work out of home offices and use computer modems and networks to send and receive materials electronically. They may go into the office only on occasion for meetings and gathering information. Freelancers and contract workers may work at a company's premises or at home.

Although the standard workweek is 40 hours, many technical writers and editors frequently work 50 or 60 hours a week. Job interruptions, meetings, and conferences can prevent writers from having long periods of time to write. Therefore, many writers work after hours or bring work home. Both writers and editors frequently work in the evening or on weekends to meet a deadline.

In many companies there is pressure to produce documents as quickly as possible. Both technical writers and editors may feel at times that they are compromising the quality of their work due to the need to conform to time and budget constraints. In some companies, technical writers and editors may have increased workloads due to company reorganizations or downsizing. They may need to do the work that was formerly done by more than one person. Technical writers and editors also are increasingly assuming roles and responsibilities formerly performed by other people and this can increase work pressures and stress.

Despite these pressures, most technical writers and editors gain immense satisfaction from their work and the roles that they perform in producing technical communications.

OUTLOOK

The writing and editing field is generally very competitive. Each year, there are more people trying to enter this field than there are available openings. The field of technical writing and editing, though, offers more opportunities than other areas of writing and editing, such as book publishing or journalism. Employment opportunities for technical writers are expected to grow faster than the average for all occupations through 2016; little or no change is expected in the employment of editors (although opportunities for technical editors should be slightly better than those for general editors). Demand is growing for technical writers who can produce well-written computer manuals. In addition to the computer industry, the pharmaceutical industry is showing an increased need for technical writers. Rapid growth in the high-technology and electronics industries and the Internet will create a continuing demand for people to write users' guides, instruction manuals, and training materials. Technical writers will be needed to produce copy that describes developments and discoveries in law, science, and technology for a more general audience.

Writers may find positions that include duties in addition to writing. A growing trend is for companies to use writers to run a department, supervise other writers, and manage freelance writers and outside contractors. In addition, many writers are acquiring responsibilities that include desktop publishing and print production coordination.

The demand for technical writers and editors is significantly affected by the economy. During recessionary times, technical writers and editors are often among the first to be laid off. Many companies today are continuing to downsize or reduce their number of employees and are reluctant to keep writers on staff. Such companies prefer to hire writers and editors on a temporary contractual basis, using them only as long as it takes to complete an assigned document. Technical writers and editors who work on a temporary or freelance basis need to market their services and continually look for new assignments. They also do not have the security or benefits offered by full-time employment.

FOR MORE INFORMATION

For information on writing and editing careers in the field of communications, contact

National Association of Science Writers
PO Box 890
Hedgesville, WV 25427-0890
Tel: 304-754-5077
http://www.nasw.org

For information on careers, contact

Society for Technical Communication
901 North Stuart Street, Suite 904
Arlington, VA 22203-1822
Tel: 703-522-4114
Email: stc@stc.org
http://www.stc.org

Index